One on One with Second Language Writers

A Guide for Writing Tutors, Teachers, and Consultants

DUDLEY W. REYNOLDS
Carnegie Mellon University–Qatar

Ann Arbor
University of Michigan Press

To Marlaine, عيوني و حياتي

To Alexander and Camille, may you inherit a world
where people can talk across languages.

Contents

Introduction

Around tables in writing centers, in our offices, and outside our classroom doors, we work with student writers one on one. During these often brief encounters, we listen to their questions, we probe, we model, and sometimes we direct. Although these one-on-one encounters are not scripted around curricular goals or learning outcomes, they probably contribute more to the development of their writing abilities than any of the activities that we plan for them because they are personalized and responsive to individual needs. For these encounters to be truly successful, however, we must be prepared. This means being knowledgeable of what it means to write and the factors that make writing more and less effective. We must also know our students—the issues that are likely to be problematic for them, the experiences that may shape their hypotheses, and their potential goals.

This book recognizes that for many of us—whether we are undergraduate consultants working in a writing center, new first-year composition teachers, or experienced English teachers encountering changing demographics in our classroom—second language writers are a group of students that we simply do not know. We may not have learned to write advanced academic papers in a second language, so we feel uncomfortable generalizing from our experiences. If we learned to write primarily by doing it, we may feel more confident talking about what writing should look like than how you get there. Finally, we may see language as distinct from writing and feel unprepared to teach the former.

This book focuses on the body of knowledge that we need to be able to think on our feet, recognize needs, and steer conversations in productive directions when working with second language writers. The guide provides tips about activities that you might adapt to your own contexts, authentic writing samples to role-play how you would handle, and lists of useful knowledge to refer to.

Chapter 1 proposes a series of questions that can be used to determine where to start. Subsequent chapters progress from macro issues like understanding the writer's background and the task at hand to more technical issues like helping second language students with organization, language choice, syntax, and punctuation. Chapter 8 then returns to the issue of how to manage the interaction and make it as productive as possible for the long run. Although the chapters are sequenced, they are intended to be stand-alone units. So read the book cover to cover, or flip to a chapter that seems especially useful for your situation.

Chapters talk about some of the distinctive factors that may influence the way learners write, the craft of writing, and the details of English sentence and discourse structure that may be causing those words and phrases to get in your way. Each chapter includes consulting tips and examples from student essays. The essays were written by actual language learners and are ones I have collected over more than 15 years of teaching. Because it is impossible to go back and contact all of the writers to ask for permission, I have changed all names of people and places to ensure anonymity. Unless otherwise indicated, the texts are reproduced here as they were submitted.

In preparing these materials, I have written from my own experience as an applied linguist, a researcher, and as someone who has taught and learned from second language writers for more than 20 years. I have tried not to assume, however, that the readers of the book will have extensive training in either composition studies or language and linguistics. I recognize that for many people, working with second language writers seems like a daunting task, and my hope is that this book may give them more confidence to work with a group of individuals who have enriched my life in so many ways.

Because this is a book written from experience, I owe incredible debts to the organizations that have supported my work and the people who have been my colleagues, students, and teachers. This project began while I was teaching at the University of Houston where I benefitted tremendously from discussions with my colleagues Tamara Fish and James Kastely, students in the master's in Applied English Linguistics program, the first-year composition teaching assistants, and the staff of the U.H. Writing Center, most notably Jennifer Wilson, Kyung-Hee Bae, Mary Gray, and Marjorie Chadwick. I have continued to learn from my inspiring colleagues at Carnegie Mellon University—Danielle Zawodny Wetzel, David Kaufer, Suguru Ishizaki, Dick Tucker, Amal Al-Malki, Silvia Pessoa, and Andreas Karatsolis. Most important, I thank the Qatar Foundation for Education, Science and Community Development for its generous support of my research and its belief in a new kind of global education. Finally, I thank my students who have shared their work and their lives with me and, in particular, those anonymous students whose papers comprise the sample essays for this book.

How to Use This Book

This book is intended as a professional development tool for anyone who conferences with individual students about their writing, particularly when the students are writing in a second language. The organization of the chapters in the book suggests a general approach to the writing conference, beginning with planning questions and strategies (Chapter 1), then addressing more macro issues related to the past experiences of the student (Chapter 2) and the academic and rhetorical goals of the assignment (Chapter 3)—both of which should help us determine specific and appropriate goals for the conference. The focus then shifts to understanding the actual writing of the students, beginning with organization (Chapter 4) and language flow (Chapter 5) and followed by syntax (Chapter 6) and punctuation (Chapter 7). The final chapter presents a set of general goals to keep in mind when conferencing with second language writers.

The book is appropriate for use in university and secondary school writing centers, teacher training programs for both general composition and ESOL instructors, and as an individual reference tool. In addition to the general discussion of issues outlined, it provides tutoring/teaching tips at the end of sections throughout the book as well as multiple examples of student writing that illustrate the various issues but that may also be discussed as general samples. The book uses non-technical language, although terminology is introduced where it might be helpful when conferencing with students. A glossary of terms is included, as is a list of useful resources.

Suggestions as to how the book might be used in particular contexts follow.

Writing Centers

Whether a writing center employs undergraduates, graduate students, or professional staff as consultants, all benefit from an introduction to the needs of second language writers. This book

may be integrated into both pre-service and in-service professional development programs. As a resource for a pre-service
workshop or training session, focus on the general principles contained in Chapters 1 and 8, which could be introduced through a
handout or slide presentation and supplemented with an
overview of the book as a whole so that participants could come
back to it at a later date. If time permits, it would also be helpful
to choose one or two of the writing samples for discussion. Good
possibilities might be the essay on page 26 by a Japanese immigrant to the United States about how she learned English and
then the proposal for a course on citizenship written by an Arab
student on page 64. They are complete essays but relatively short
and offer the opportunity to discuss a range of issues. A key goal
for the discussion should be to move participants past the initial
tendency to focus on surface-level grammatical errors and instead
to have them identify overall strengths of the writing and ways
that it could be improved from the macro level.

In-service training programs typically allow more time for
working with a resource. Each chapter could be the basis for a
series of weekly discussions addressing the needs of second language writers in the writing center, for example. If this much time
is not available, the content could be divided into an introduction
to the writing conference (Chapters 1 and 8), overview of writers
and readers (Chapters 2 and 3), macro-level writing issues (Chapters 4 and 5), and surface-level issues (Chapters 6 and 7). In addition to discussing the designated topics, participants could be
asked to demonstrate some of the teaching tips or to bring in
copies of student papers that they think relate to the issues being
discussed. Participants might also role play conferences using
some of the sample texts. As advocated in Chapter 8, encourage
participants to think not only in terms of immediate activities and
responses but also in terms of long-range learning outcomes for
individual students.

Additionally, a list of Useful Resources begins on page 150.
These are general reference materials that would be helpful to
have in a writing center. They also provide more in-depth treat-

ments of specific topics and so might be appropriate to ask individual tutors to report on as part of an in-service training.

Teacher Training Programs

Second language writers typically study in composition classes taught either by instructors with a background in English studies or TESOL. This book could serve as a course reading for a composition pedagogy course. It could be studied as part of a separate unit on second language writers, or instructors might wish to consider assigning particular chapters in conjunction with other readings covering similar topics but addressing the needs of native speakers. In this way, students could be encouraged to consider what the unique needs of second language writers are with respect to standard curricular goals. It would also be useful to extend the discussion of the book to considering its implications for making written comments on student papers and grading them.

For a course on second language writing in a master's in TESOL program, the book can be used in conjunction with a textbook or selection of articles as a way of framing issues related to second language writers. One goal for including it should be to focus particular attention on conferencing as an instructional approach, a topic that is not explicitly covered in many course books on second language writing. Chapters 1–3 and 8 may be most useful in this regard. Articles written from the perspectives of sociocultural theory and/or interaction theory could be paired with the book since both of these theories about language learning focus on the benefits of individualized interaction. Because the book is intended to be accessible for individuals without expertise in applied linguistics, explicit references to the literature on each of the topics discussed are not provided. One potential activity, therefore, might be to ask students to prepare literature reviews for topics covered in different chapters. Because this book is written for a wider audience than ESOL specialists, it may be useful to consider as part of discussions what it means to target the improvement of writing as opposed to the improvement of language and how those assumptions inform the guidance provided by the book.

Individual Use

The book is a useful resource to share with individual instructors across disciplines who may be asking, "How do I help these second language students?" The premise of the book is that individuals who are working one-on-one with a student should be prepared to identify issues and envision ways to help on the spot. They may benefit from having handouts that they can distribute as resources or activities to roll out when the need arises, but first and foremost they must also be able to think on their feet. The best way to prepare for these situations is to explore issues and consider scenarios in advance—in short, to feel informed to make decisions.

Whether you read this book cover to cover or on a casual basis, it will contribute to the confidence needed to work one-on-one with student writers.

Where Do I Start?

Ming has just walked in for her writing conference and handed you a two-page, neat draft of the first assignment. She's very quiet and doesn't say much; she just looks at you as if she expects you to say something profound about her paper. She expects help, whether you are the instructor, a tutor, or writing center consultant. Not wanting to let her down, you pick up the paper, grab a pen just in case you need to put a dot over something to discuss later, and you start reading. Pretty soon though, you find that you're making marks on every line and that it's increasingly difficult to get the gist of her sentences. The more you read, the more confused you become. Little beads of sweat appear on your forehead, and you wonder, "Where do I start?"

The first step is to put the pen down. I know, you just want to use it to identify words or passages that cause you problems as a reader. You've been trained as a writing consultant or teacher, and you know better than to try to correct grammar or mark language errors on a first read. But the pen is a warning sign! (So is the urge to pick one up.) It means that you are trying to read in too many ways at once.

Reading researchers generally talk about two complementary strategies for deciphering a text, top-down and bottom-up. Top-down strategies focus on the overall meaning, building an evolving model for the message of the text that is used to figure out new pieces of the puzzle. Bottom-up strategies focus on the meaning of individual words and infer new meanings from what is known about patterns for stringing words together. If we are reading for enjoyment, we usually employ both approaches. We like descriptive language, and so we savor it, noticing the particular turning of a phrase. At the same time, if it's fiction, we keep in mind the plot structure, or if it's an opinion essay, we keep in mind the stated purpose. We notice a word like *seem* or other hedging devices because they cast doubt on the veracity of a character, but we also count how many valid points have been made and whether we've likely reached the clincher of the essay yet.

Sometimes, however, we need to use one approach more than the other. If we have 75 pages of a U.S. history textbook to finish tonight, we tend to do a lot of top-down reading. We look in places where we expect to find key sentences, like the end of the introductory paragraph and the beginning of body paragraphs; we string them together, and we see if we have a coherent product that will get us through tomorrow's lecture. At other times we are faced with a text that might as well be written in a foreign language. For me, the fine print on the back of a credit card application is a good example. I cannot skim it because the vocabulary is specialized, there's a comma every five words setting off a qualification of the preceding five words, and there are a lot more nouns and prepositions than verbs. Because I don't want to miss any details, I use careful bottom-up processing strategies to piece the text together.

Why does my reading strategy matter? Ming is an English language learner. At first, her essay may seem like a good candidate for bottom-up reading. Words and phrases jump out at you as you start to read it. Some of them just seem odd; some of them make the alarm bell on your high school English teacher's desk start to ring; and some of them make you want to laugh. The problem with bottom-up reading at this point, however, is that it distracts you from your job, which is to offer Ming a plan to improve the essay as a whole and become a better writer in general. You may need to force yourself to read Ming's essay from the top down. Get the big picture first, and then focus on the details.

This book offers strategies and useful information to help you accomplish both of these tasks—looking at the big picture and providing support for the details—during a conference or tutoring session with a second language writer. Chapter 1 discusses a general strategy for approaching texts written by English language learners.

Initial Questions to Ask

As you begin the process of reading an essay from the top down, I propose six questions to keep in mind. They are intended to help you consider a range of variables that may affect the essay's ability to communicate a message and its ultimate effectiveness.

1. Do I understand the general point of the essay?

Writing teachers use many terms to describe the general point of an essay: *thesis statement, controlling idea, focus point, statement of purpose, main idea,* etc. Regardless of the terminology, most of us agree that one of the defining characteristics of shorter pieces of academic writing is a singularity of focus. Different types of writing vary in the degree to which this focus is made explicit and whether the focus represents a purpose, a feeling, or simply an entity to be described.

In this book's introduction, I began the third paragraph with *This book focuses on . . .* , followed by sentences describing the contents of the book as a whole. When we use words like *focus* or *I will argue,* we are using **metadiscourse to explicitly mark a central point.** In U.S. academic texts we also often rely on our readers' expectations about location to signal that a sentence represents a central idea. In the composition class essay, the thesis statement is typically the last sentence of the first paragraph. In a business plan, the opening paragraph should name the entity being described and outline the way it will be described.

Were I writing up an ethnographic study of peer tutoring sessions, however, I might begin with a lengthy illustrative narrative and leave it for the reader to derive the point. If I decided to state a purpose, I might delay it until the end, like the moral to a fable. Essays in popular magazines such as *Time* or *Newsweek* often employ this strategy, ending with nothing more than a question for the reader to think about.

Newspaper stories, on the other hand, tend to begin with the juiciest details of a story—the body count or how many billions were embezzled—and then they move into the background information. Although media critics can often detect a journalist's point of view through looking at what details were highlighted or the tenor of descriptive words, the point of view is rarely made explicit in a single sentence.

Just as types of writing vary with respect to where and how clearly the focus is presented, there is also some evidence that different cultures may vary in their preferences for how the focus is presented. U.S. academic culture seems to value explicit, up-front statements about where a paper is going. (Keep in mind that instructors often try to liven up an assignment by asking students to write an academic paper in the guise of a non-academic genre, such as a letter or a position brief for which there are different expectations.) Apologists for the writing styles of other academic cultures note that the up-front preference doesn't really allow the reader a chance to make up his or her own mind or reach independent conclusions. In other words, the U.S. preference places the burden of interpretation primarily on the writer; the reader's job is to take it as given and then make a judgment about the package.

This is a gross oversimplification of the reading process, but I think you get my point. When working with a second language writer, you need to entertain the possibility that there is a singularity of focus, but that it's just not presented in the way you expected. Of course, with a writer from any culture, there is always the possibility that there isn't a central point. If that's the case, you know what to do. You work with the student to identify the different threads and then decide whether to choose one and throw out the rest or to look for an idea that ties everything together.

Finally, you also have to ask whether the focus is meaningful. I try to stay away from topics asking students to compare U.S. culture with theirs, and one of the reasons is because I find that too many students try to make their papers coherent under the rubric of *There are many similarities/differences/similarities and differences between my country and the United States.* This can work as the controlling statement for an essay, but the essay is going to be boring, and at the end I'm going to be left wondering why this essay was worth my time.

> **Tutoring / Teaching Tip**
>
> Make a collection of different types of texts, some with explicitly stated purposes and some with implicit. Ask the student to summarize the author's purpose for each text in one sentence. This can also lead to good discussions about the difference between *topic* and *purpose*.

2. Do I think the essay fits the goal(s) of the assignment?

A second factor is the social context for which the paper was written. I'm assuming that most of the writing you see will be an assignment for an academic class, but within academia there is a diverse range of writing types. Composition classes typically focus on the essay and the research paper, but other classes may require book reports, reading reaction papers, position statements, or proposals. Some non-humanities classes ask for written notes on observations, experiments, and field experiences. For students to be successful at producing any one of these types, they need to be aware of a broad range of conventions related to content, organization, language formality, and audience recognition.

These conventions can be a problem for any student. But if most of the writing you have done involved summarizing what you read in order to show content mastery or you immigrated to the United States in the tenth grade and spent most of your time since then learning to write the kinds of essays needed to pass standardized tests, then you may not even be aware of what you don't know. You may also be afraid to demonstrate your lack of knowledge by asking the teacher for help. Even if the teacher is nice and gives you a sample paper, you may not have the linguistic awareness necessary to notice the conventions in it.

If you are working with this student as a writing consultant, you have to think about more than what the piece of writing means to you; you also have to think about how it will be received elsewhere. This may involve some detective work on your part. Of course, you want to see anything the teacher has given the student related to the assignment—instructions, lists of potential resources, grading procedures, and, if you're lucky, examples. You also want to query the student about what he or she thinks is expected. Does the student have a clear idea? How important does he or she think the assignment is? Can the student articulate these things clearly?

With respect to conventions for the assignment genre, you may want to consider formal properties first, things like:

- What kind of title, if any, does the genre typically have?
- Does it have a fixed organizational structure?
- Does it use headings to mark the structure?
- What are the parameters for length?
- If it includes citations, what style format is used?

You will also need to think about more intangible characteristics though. One area that can be particularly problematic for students from other educational cultures is the incorporation of source material. I have had students who worked quite hard to piece together as many quotations as possible from a large number of sources and yet never said what they thought about the topic. Others have taken nicely worded phrases and even entire sentences from a book and blended them into a paragraph without ever using quotation marks. They acknowledged the book in their bibliography and freely admitted that they had used it to help write the section. When I told the students that the teacher was probably more interested in seeing that they understood the source material well enough to form an independent opinion about it, though, they were genuinely surprised. They thought they had.

The issue of how outside authorities are treated within a genre is related to what composition teachers refer to as **voice**. Voice is often treated as the way in which individualism is expressed in a piece of writing. A number of second language writing researchers have noted that asking a student to express voice may be particularly problematic if the student comes from a collectivist culture where the good of society is typically valued over individual needs and desires. The issue here is more than whether it's OK to use *I* when we write, however, because there are many U.S. academic genres where first person pronouns are avoided completely. Rather, this has to do with the willingness to take an individual stand and to talk about other authors in a way that acknowledges that you see things differently from them.

When working with second language writers, I tend to avoid the collectivist versus individualistic debate because I think it will inevitably lead to confrontation and us/them dichotomies. Instead I talk about voice in a more metaphorical sense, such as whether the writer has a sense of the text as part of a discourse. In other words, does the writer have a sense of who he or she is talking to and the language needed to be understood? With academic assignments, a big question is always whether the audience is the teacher (who knows what the assignment was), a generic reader who cannot be assumed to know anything about the assignment or the writer, or a specified reader such as the board of directors for an imaginary company. In order to engage in a conversation with the target audience, is it better to use a casual, conversational style or to demonstrate technical precision in the choice of words and syntactic structures?

As you can see, even this notion of voice is somewhat fuzzy. You probably are very good at it though, and your expertise is the product of experience. Second

Tutoring / Teaching Tip

Question 2 relates to the student's ability to analyze audience. Sometimes it's helpful to make this process explicit by giving the student a chart to fill in about the reader(s) for whatever he or she is working on. The chart can include questions like: Who is the audience? What are they likely to know about your topic? What are they likely to feel or believe about your topic? Make two rows in the chart—one for before reading and one for after. This also communicates the message that writing should be transformative—that is, readers' beliefs or states of knowledge should be different after they finish reading.

language writers are typically playing catch up; they do not have the benefit of knowledge built up over years. They need input from someone who can see their writing in a broader context, who knows that MLA and APA reference styles are different but who also knows whether the teacher's question should be restated in the introductory paragraph of an essay exam.

3. Do I recognize an organizational strategy? Is it effective?

It's been my experience that students rarely hand in a paper that is not organized. If you think about it, it is genuinely difficult to tell a story where the events don't occur in order. With argumentative writing, it is possible to begin with the logical conclusion and then express your reasons for reaching that conclusion, or you can save the punch line until the end. Whether a text's organization is apparent, however, is another matter. And whether it is effective is yet another.

I probably should define what I mean by organization. Essentially I understand organization to comprise two abilities: the ability to cluster ideas hierarchically and the ability to sequence those clusters in an order that produces a desired effect in a reader. When we read a text, we start with the default assumption that the ideas in a sentence are related to the ideas of the preceding sentence and the successive sentence. This is especially clear with narratives where we assume that the order in which events are related matches the order in which they occurred unless the writer explicitly indicates otherwise. With expository writing, we do not make assumptions about order of occurrence, but we still expect relatedness of content or purpose.

With the exception of very basic texts such as a written invitation or phone message, however, mere relatedness is not sufficient. Most written texts involve a more complex association of ideas than the phone message, and readers need help if they are expected to process those ideas efficiently. The devices we have in English for making organizational hierarchy and sequencing explicit are metadiscourse and paragraphs.

Metadiscourse includes markers like those previously mentioned signaling a statement of purpose, transitional words and phrases such as *in addition* or *on the other hand*, and headings, which essentially provide the reader with an outline. Metadiscourse is a universal feature of language. Language learners have to master nuances such as the difference between *furthermore* and *moreover* (try explaining that one!), but the concept of organizational words will not seem strange.

In contrast to metadiscourse, paragraphs are not a universal phenomenon in written languages, and conventions about their importance and what a paragraph includes vary even more. Beginning second language writers will often write an essay as one long paragraph or set apart each sentence as if it were a separate paragraph. This may result from how texts are segmented in their native language, or it may be that they are so focused on word choice and sentence construction that paragraphing seems relatively unimportant.

Readers of English have a lot of expectations for the paragraph though. Unless the text is in a newspaper or dialogue in a novel, they probably expect it to fill up a certain amount of space on the page. They don't expect it to fill up more than a page, however! They also look for a sentence, generally at the beginning of the paragraph, that signals what it will be about and also how it fits into the text as a whole. (Again, the presence of explicit topic sentences varies by text type.) Finally, they expect the paragraph's content to be internally coherent and for the paragraph as a whole to cohere to the paragraphs before and after. Sometimes, you may need to ask a student directly what he or she knows about paragraphs.

If a student has mastered the art of chunking information into paragraph-size units, then you need to consider whether the organization of the units is effective. Developing writers too often conceive of the body of a work as the place where points are listed. The result is what I call the "grocery list" essay; it has lots of ingredients, but it needs some preparation before a reader can digest it. The preparation involves establishing a flow to the ideas, of reconceptualizing the points as the pieces of a puzzle or boxes in a schematic drawing. In short, thinking of organization as more than physical location.

"Grocery list" essays often appear in the guise of a generic five-paragraph academic essay. This format is a peculiarly U.S. institution, but many second language writers have been introduced to it by an English teacher somewhere who wanted them to have a safe formula for passing standardized writing assessments. For a student already grappling with sentence structure and lexical choice, ready-made structure is a godsend, and it may well be sufficient to get them through the standardized tests. Unfortunately, the format is often presented in the context of a power relationship also—that is, "If you want to write like Americans, then you have to. . . ." Whether driven by futility or utility, the writers rarely interpret the suggestion to include three body paragraphs as anything more than a directive to brainstorm three aspects of a topic and develop each one into a paragraph. They cluster ideas, but they do not really pay attention to sequencing them.

Sentence structure and lexical choice may always be problematic for second language writers because they are properties of the second language, and that does not come easily. But organization is not the property of a language. When we talk about the organization of a piece of writing, we are discussing the ordering and juxtaposition of mental constructs stored by the human mind independently from language (or at least most researchers believe this to be true). As such, organization is the one aspect of writing where second language writers have the best chances for success. It is worth our time to figure out

> **Tutoring / Teaching Tip**
>
> One way to teach sequencing is to take a hard copy of the student's paper, physically cut the paragraphs apart, and then rearrange them. (You can also cut paragraphs into sentences.) Ask the student whether the essay is better or the same as a result of the rearrangement. If the student replies that it does not make a difference, explain that it should. If the student argues that the paragraphs cannot be rearranged, ask him or her to justify that claim by referring to both language and content.

the structure they are employing, reflect on its effectiveness, and help them play to its strength.

4. Is the writing interesting?

One of the main reasons I advocate starting with a top-down approach to reading second language writers' texts is that the bottom-up approach too often leads to a piece of writing that is technically correct but boring. In U.S. academia, we measure the effectiveness of writing using constructs like clarity of focus, development of ideas, and mechanical accuracy. Outside of academics, the effectiveness of writing is measured by whether it can sustain a reader's interest long enough to communicate a message.

So, how do we make a text interesting? There is an entire genre of books identified by the subtitle: *A Guide to Effective Writing*. Most of these books include instructions like avoid generic vocabulary (e.g., *something*), use active verbs instead of passive, and beware of too many convoluted noun phrases. If we are writing a personal essay about the joys and difficulties of being a full-time student and working many hours, this is good advice. Heavy noun phrases require extra mental commitment to process, and generic vocabulary does not engender the rich image that many people like to paint. This is bad advice, however, if you are writing a legal brief, a concise summary for an annotated bibliography, or a write-up of a lab experiment.

What makes a text interesting varies with the purpose of the text and the characteristics of the typical reader. It may evolve from the eloquence of the language, the novelty of the argument, or the ability to draw together in one place a number of different source texts. If the text is a type where personal experiences can be included in the content, then second language writers often have an advantage when it comes to novelty. They can incorporate experiences and viewpoints that do not seem commonplace to a U.S. reader. With other types of writing, they will have to work as hard as anyone else to make the text interesting.

What is important when working with second language writers is to stress that good writing is more than technical precision; it is more than getting the language "right." We can tell a U.S.-educated writer that his or her style is verbose or pedantic; the same can be true for a non-U.S.-educated writer. We owe it to our students to be honest and always to keep in mind that the role of writing is effective communication. We also need to keep in mind that what constitutes effective communication is variable.

5. How bothered am I by the language? Am I bothered in spite of what the essay says or because I can't understand what the writer is saying?

In advocating a top-down approach, I am not suggesting that we can totally ignore language structure and choice. You can put the pen down, but it is unrealistic to expect you not to notice the missing *it* or that you had to read one sentence three times before you reached an interpretation that would allow you to continue reading. The trick is not to let these types of things bog you down or prevent you from considering the issues previously discussed. You also have to begin thinking about how and when you will address the language issues.

Many second language writers have studied English since early childhood and although there are a few features that mark them as non-native writers—sentences like *I wondered who is the teacher looking for*—language issues are not common in their writing. With this kind of writer, you want to focus on more general writing concerns. In fact, where their language differs from the structure you would choose may be what is known in second language acquisition studies as a **fossilized** structure. Fossilized structures are generally impervious to instruction and are likely to be used by the learner for the rest of his or her life. You can suggest that the writer make a list of structures to check for when editing the final paper, but beyond this, it is probably not going to be very helpful to spend a lot of time talking about the ins and outs of the grammar.

There are other writers, however, for whom we have to acknowledge that their use of language bothers us. In these cases, you need to do some soul searching. Do the language problems primarily feel like a nuisance to you? If so, it probably means that you like the message of the text and are generally satisfied with the way it is presented. If that's the case, then it may be appropriate to begin working on language issues fairly early. Do some prioritizing, identify the issues that are most frequent, give the learner a chance to self-correct, and then try to explain if need be.

In other cases, however, you may feel that an essay is rife with grammatical errors to the point that you are not always sure what the writer is saying. The human instinct at this point is to bring out the grammar charts and launch right into myriad explanations about the technicalities of English articles or the meaning of the preposition *at*. This is probably the wrong direction to go. If you are having difficulty understanding what the writer intended, then it is likely that the writer was not sure either. Second language learners rarely display 100 percent consistency in their paradigms for features like word order, agreement, and grammatical inflection. Sometimes they produce what sound like perfect constructions; other times they surprise us with mismatches in structures we assumed they had mastered. Most scholars agree that the mismatches can be induced by cognitive burden: They are more likely to mess up the grammar if they are still trying to work out what they want to say.

If this describes the student you are working with, then you need to spend a lot of time talking about purpose for writing, audience expectations, and organization first. Once the student has worked his or her ideas into a coherent presentation, turn to the linguistic choices that were made. This is the chronology that matches the path a text takes from our brains to paper. It is also a more efficient way to address language issues. If you start by working on language issues because you feel overwhelmed by them, then you may spend an inordinate amount of time talking about a structure in a sentence that will or should never make it into the final draft.

6. What is the strongest aspect of the writing?

This final question applies regardless of the student you are working with. Everyone needs a pat on the back, especially if a student has come to you for help, because this probably indicates some insecurity about writing. In addition, presumably our goal as writing consultants and teachers is to help the students we work with become better writers, to help them develop their abilities to communicate and influence. Implicit in the notion of development is building, and it is hard to build if what we are doing is tearing apart. Yes, we may need to point out where some reconstruction is necessary, but we also need to point out where towers can be erected.

Some second language writers may be very insecure about their writing. As a result they may stick to simple grammatical structures, stereotypical examples, and lots of dictionary-derived vocabulary. Others are risk takers. They know they are going to make mistakes, and so they do not worry about making them. They write with abandon. Sometimes they come up with a piece that is very creative; at other times they attempt a level of complexity beyond what their language capabilities can handle. Although for different reasons, both of these types of writers need you to point out what's good in their essays.

The play-it-safe writers need the challenges that come from attempting more complex forms of expression. If they mention a festival in their culture but do not provide any details about it, they need to know you are interested in other cultures and their practices. That encouragement might lead them to try a passage full of descriptive adjectives and relative clauses. It also introduces the idea that readers have likes and dislikes.

With reckless-abandon writers, on the other hand, you want to point out the potential benefits of trying something they are not sure they can handle. Let them know you recognize that they tried to express a very difficult argument. You also want to help them channel their energy. Let them know what works, whether it is a hypothetical argument or a flashback scene as the introduction to a persuasive paper. Suggest another point in the paper to try the same technique.

The acquisition of a language's grammar involves a lot of experimentation. Learners hear a structure, think they have a general idea how it functions, try it out, and then re-evaluate their understanding based on whether or not it seemed to work. They generally will continue using it as long as no one starts saying, "What did you say?" (Note that they rarely have someone telling them, "Don't say it that way.") Grammatical competence develops through this process of hearing, trying, and evaluating the feedback.

I think competence in writing develops in the same manner. Learners develop their initial ideas about the functions and types of writing through the texts they are exposed to. They may then attempt some of these types. They need feedback in order to continue though. Unlike spoken communication, writing can be an impersonal act, especially in academia where too often students receive papers back with little more than a grade and possibly some negative generalizations if the grade needs to be justified. Our job is to communicate what works and to provide feedback that promotes growth.

ESL Writers: Background

One of my greatest concerns in writing is a desire not to generalize in this book. In the first chapter, I used *second language writers* eleven times, *students* ten times, and *language learners* two times. Every time I used one of these collective phrases, I risked the implication that a group of individuals as diverse as Henry Kissinger, Celine Dion, and your student Ming should be expected to have the same needs and abilities just because English is not the language they learned from their parents. Every person you work with is first and foremost an individual. That said, generalizations can also be helpful. By virtue of birth or experience, individuals may be influenced by the culture of a particular ethnic group, social class, academic milieu, or worldview. The more you know about the common beliefs and experiences that define a culture, the better prepared you are to interact with representatives of that culture. You have a starting point for devising a course of instruction.

Perceptions of You

One place to start when considering generalizations that we can make about cultural groups is with ourselves. Odds are that the students you work with have just as many preconceptions about you as you have about them. One important generalization has to do with your role as a tutor/instructor/giver of advice. If you view writing as a collaborative process, then you may be trying to establish a "peer" relationship. This is easier for you because it does not force you to be an "expert," and it also allows you to pass the buck when it comes to enforcing things like deadlines or the consequences of plagiarism. However, if the student you are working with has been schooled outside the United States, then the notion of going to a peer for instruction may seem really strange because a peer is not an expert.

In the United States, most students are accustomed to learning and receiving academic support from a variety of sources. In group projects, we teach each other. We talk with counselors on a first name basis, sit on the grass with our graduate teaching assistants, and make late-night visits to learning support services. In many educational cultures, however, instruction is primarily the responsibility of the educated "experts"—the people with PhDs. Even if you do not have a PhD (and especially if you do), you may find students approaching you with an air of respect and deference. They think of you as an "expert." This can be flattering, but it can also be problematic if you are trying to challenge them to think for themselves. Sometimes we really have to play devil's advocate if we want them to do something other than acquiesce to our opinions.

Students' preconceptions can also extend to what they think you will believe. Internationally, the United States is often perceived as a country of individualists more concerned about their psychological well-being than the physical needs of others. Americans are also sometimes thought of as ideological to the point of naiveté. Yet another stereotype is that we know very little about other cultures or languages. This may be felt especially among immigrant students who have experienced the pressure to assimilate and frequently encounter what seem to them like very ignorant questions about their country or culture.

These preconceptions are important because they may influence what students think they should or should not write in an essay. One of the most extreme examples I have encountered of this has been when, on two or three occasions, I have had students assume that it would be acceptable to me if they included derogatory remarks about African Americans in an essay. That one culture could hold prejudiced views about another did not surprise me, but I was surprised and at first wounded that those students thought it would be acceptable to share those prejudices with me. But then I realized that, for them, I was a white male from the southern part of the United States. From past experiences, I also knew that television mini-series about the U.S. Civil War were immensely popular in some countries. Consciously or subconsciously, they probably associated me with the stereotypical white plantation owner.

When working with a student, it can be helpful to spend some time discussing the student's general beliefs and opinions about a topic. When you do, though, you may find the student expressing ideas that seem to contradict statements made in the writing about which you are conferencing. This may be a sign that the student has tried too hard to accommodate his or her perceptions of the intended audience. If this is the case, you need to point out the contradiction and suggest that it is hard to be convincing if you are not writing from conviction. You may also find a student who nonchalantly makes remarks that you consider patently offensive. This is a sign that the student does not know enough about the audience and that you need to provide this information. One of the real joys of working with diverse student populations is the opportunity to share ideas and opinions in such a way that everyone's horizons are broadened. You are part of students' educational experiences, and very often they need you to make explicit what no one else will.

Significance of Prior Education

As we move into generalizations about students and the characteristics of their writing, one useful piece of information to find out is whether they have received some of their education in local schools or whether all of it was outside the United States. The latter group is often referred to as "visa students," and for many years, these were the students that most people thought of as "ESL writers." These are the students identified by most colleges and universities as "international students." They are either undergraduate or graduate students who received their previous degree (secondary or bachelor's) from an international institution, have to apply through the international admissions office, and are required to take a test of English proficiency such as the TOEFL® or IELTS™. Depending on their level of English proficiency, they may enter the university directly or after studying for a year in a university Intensive English Program.

When these students enter the university, they are often tracked during their first or second semester into a non-native section of first-year composition. (International graduate students sometimes end up in these courses as well.) These courses were originally created at many universities because faculty recognized that the linguistic patterns characteristic of international student writing were distinct from those of "native" students and based on the assumption that a composition course was a good place for a crash introduction to the university's academic culture. I won't argue whether a composition course is a good place to explore culture, but I will say I think it is appropriate to talk about culture with visa students early on because that is when many of them are dealing with culture shock.

Visa students are constantly reminded by little things—like having to ask for no ice in their water or the fact that everyone in their dorm closes their doors—that they are "different." They are at a point where they see people and systems as "American" or "Pakistani" or "Latin." When it comes to socializing with others, they will likely seek out people with whom they feel a shared experience, and that means other international students and, if possible, international students from their native country. As a result, some dormitories on larger university campus often begin looking (and sounding) more like an international student cooperative than the melting pot that they are intended to be. In short, everything around these students leads them to dichotomize the world into us versus them and "our way" versus "your way." You will often see this dichotomization spilling over into their writing, and you may need to work with them on avoiding broad generalizations and blanket assumptions. You may also want to consider whether questions you ask them (e.g., *How do you do this in your country?*) or assumptions you make about their beliefs or interests are contributing to their feelings of alienation.

Finally, visa students often represent the intellectual and/or economic elite of their native countries. Because they are not citizens or permanent residents, they generally pay the highest tuition rates and are not eligible for government scholarships. In the United States, visa regulations further stipulate that they can only work on the university campus. Thus, the funds for what can be a very expensive education, even at a public university, have to come primarily from family sources or highly competitive scholarships in their home countries. This can mean that they feel an even greater sense of obligation to succeed than most students do; it also can mean that they have never had to work hard in order to enjoy privileges.

Regardless of their work ethic, they have often had access to the best schools in their native countries, and if they have worked hard, they may have developed content knowledge well beyond the average undergraduate. They may also have an advanced awareness of what it means to be literate. They are aware that we organize language differently for different rhetorical purposes. They know that things like vocabulary and sentence structure differ significantly between conversational speech and academic writing. They may even be quite adept at employing imagery or cultural allusions. Their biggest problem, however, is applying these concepts in a foreign language.

I write *foreign* intentionally because researchers often make a distinction between *foreign* language learning and *second* language learning. Foreign language learning occurs in an environment where the language being learned is not generally used as part of everyday communication. Thus, it has to be primarily learned and practiced in a classroom. Second language learning, on the other hand, occurs in an environment where the language being learned can be used in and out of the classroom.

Just like the typical Spanish, French, or German foreign language classes, English as a foreign language (EFL) classes tend to focus on vocabulary memorization and grammar instruction. Even classes that adopt more communicative orientations, such as having students role-play specific tasks or write advertisements instead of essays, are limited to simulating authentic situations. As a result, many visa students arrive knowing a great deal about the structure of the language but never having had to use it for extensive face-to-face communication. They have never had to think on their feet, if you will, in English. This means that any type of communication (spoken or written) in which they do not have a lot of time to plan and review what they want to say or write can be difficult.

One caveat to this last generalization: in today's globalized world, it may alternatively be the case with visa students that they have in fact used English extensively outside of the language classroom. Often, however, they have encountered it in a specific setting. That setting may be an academic field such as medicine where English is frequently the language of instruction, through imported television comedy and drama shows, or as a participant in their country's tourist trade. If this is the case, then odds are that their command of English may seem unbalanced at times. They may be fluent conversationalists as long as the topic is not too esoteric, or they may be speed-readers as long as the topic uses vocabulary from their academic major.

Tutoring / Teaching Tip

If you are going to be working with a student on an ongoing basis, it is often helpful to conduct a diagnostic interview related to the student's academic and language learning background. Ask questions like, *How much reading have you done in English? What is the longest text you have ever read in English? Did you have a chance to speak English outside the classroom? Where and how often?* Your goal with these questions should be to identify the functions for which the student may be more and less comfortable using English. You can then move to saying, "It sounds like you haven't done much X. Why don't you Y." Remind the student that the key to learning a language is not just memorization, but also practice.

Generation 1.5 Students

In contrast to visa students is a group of individuals who have received at least some of their intermediate and secondary education in local school systems but whose use of English is still distinct from the majority of entering college students. These individuals are commonly referred to as **Generation 1.5** students because, like first-generation immigrants, they typically were born in another country; however, they are also like second-generation immigrants because they often lack much of the cultural knowledge held by their parents. The structural aspects of English that are inherently difficult for them to master may be the same as the aspects that are difficult for a visa student, but their past encounters with literacy tasks and with English make them quite a different population to work with.

It is impossible to generalize about why these students may have immigrated to an English-speaking country other than to say that they (or their parents) thought their lives would be better in the new place. Often this is an indication that they have been somehow marginalized in their native society and that they are less likely to come from a cultural or economic elite. Furthermore, getting started in a new country is never easy regardless of the economic resources you bring with you. Immigrant families face the stresses not only of learning a new language but also earning a living and mastering the transportation, health care, and legal systems. How they deal with these stresses can vary from putting everyone to work outside the home to having a strict job specialization where the father is the bread winner, the mother maintains the home (and the home culture), and the children serve as the bridge to mainstream culture in the new country.

For our purposes, the focus needs to be on the opportunities Generation 1.5 children have to learn English. In the past two decades, the number of what are termed in the United States "limited English proficiency" children entering public schools has increased dramatically at all grade levels. Moreover, intermediate and secondary schools are increasingly dealing with what are termed "low-literacy" students who have had their prior schooling interrupted often for a number of years and who may never have even learned to read in any language. When they enroll in their new schools, they may be offered an ESL class anywhere from one period to the whole day depending on their exact proficiency level and the school. Often these classes have to attend to the social as well as the academic needs of the students. They need to give the students the conversational skills necessary to interact with the other students in non-ESL classes; they need to teach about doctors and banks and bus routes; and they need to build the linguistic structures necessary to decipher and produce academic English—in 50 minutes per day.

Although it might seem logical to provide supplemental language instruction as long as a student needs it, more often the length of time a student can spend in an ESL program is limited by state and local regulations, and in many places, the goal is to exit a student within three years into regular language arts classes. The regular language arts classes generally include grammar lessons along with discussion of literature and practice in essay writing. The grammar lessons language learners need, however, are typically absent. Regular language arts classes tend to focus on the vocabulary of grammar (e.g., labels for parts of speech and types of clauses) and prescriptive rules (e.g., *who* versus *whom*, comma before coordinating conjunction) but omit explanations about structures that native speakers typically use without conscious thought like articles or verb tenses. If you do not have an intuitive sense that a dependent clause does not represent a complete thought, then knowing when to use commas may seem like an impossible task.

At the same time that the Generation 1.5 students are grappling with the relevance of knowing that "a noun names a person, place, thing, or idea," they are also hanging out with friends at the mall on Saturday afternoon, mixing phrases like *dyuseethat?* with *qué pasa?* picking up the latest teen magazine filled with the buzz about who's been seen with whom, grabbing a hamburger and fries at McDonald's® , and then coming home to watch "Saturday Night Live" satirize the political figures of the day. School is not easy for these students, and life is a constant mixture of old, new, and in-between.

If they are lucky, however, they will have someone pushing them to stay in school, or they will realize its economic and cognitive benefits and will persevere. They will piece together the credits necessary to pass high school and squeak by on the SAT® primarily due to their math scores. Alternatively, they may be so motivated that they excel far beyond their peers who see education as merely something to be done rather than a privilege. They may end up at a junior college, at a large public four-year urban university, or at a state institution on a scholarship for top students.

Wherever they end up, they often arrive decidedly better at spoken interaction than written. They sound like native speakers because they have mastered casual, interactional language, but they do not write like them. Because their literacy training has been spotty, they are not aware of vocabulary that occurs primarily in written texts or the fact that many types of academic writing rely on subordination and reduced clauses to pack as much information into as few words as possible. They have had only a limited exposure to the conventions of academic writing since they were in an ESL class when the other eleventh graders wrote a paper that had to cite sources. They may also not be very good at the types of structural analysis necessary to edit a piece of writing or even understand your explanations on grammatical points.

However, because they graduated from a local secondary school, they are not usually identified as non-native speakers or international students by a university. They are not required to take an English language proficiency test for admission, and they may be advised to enroll in regular composition courses instead of the ESL courses. They may also end up in disproportionate numbers in composition courses labeled as "developmental"—not ready for credit. These courses often serve as a catch-all for students who have managed to graduate from high school without ever having to write a paper longer than two pages, students who have been stigmatized as having "poor grammar" because they learned a non-prestige variety of English in their home, and students who have genuine difficulty with writing due to learning dis-abilities. Developmental writing courses typically address student needs through sustained writing practice complemented with les-sons on composing techniques and red-flag language issues, all of which are useful for Generation 1.5 students. The Generation 1.5 students, however, may need further help with linguistic structures such as articles and verb tenses that are second nature to the native-born students. They may also be wondering why they are grouped with students with whom they feel very little in common.

Whereas with visa students identity issues tend to be oversim-plified as an us/them dichotomy, with Generation 1.5 students they can be so complex that students feel lost. They cannot write a paper comparing situation comedies in Thailand and the United States because they don't remember Thai television and the U.S. shows are filled with allusions that don't ring a bell. They do not feel they belong to any culture, and they often report that they do not even have a language that they feel comfortable speaking or writing. They think they have forgotten their birth language and are constantly told that they have not yet mastered English. They may simply feel confused and lost, and this may show up in their writing.

In identifying these issues, my intent is not to make Generation 1.5 students appear to be a lost cause. Rather, I think it is impor-tant to realize the potential sources of their difficulties so that you can best address them. Understand that their command of English may be limited to casual speech, in which case it is helpful to focus their attention on differences between everyday spoken lan-guage and formal, academic language. Understand that they may have very poorly developed skills for analyzing language, requir-ing you to spend significant time helping them to pick apart example sentences and texts. Try to make them aware of gram-matical markers like -s, -ed, and *the* and where they typically occur. Finally, understand that they may not have the same access to cultural icons or history as someone who has lived in the same place all their lives, so encourage them to use writing as a tool for discovery. Suggest that writing is a way to sort out feelings and beliefs and to organize and build knowledge constructs. It's a great way to gain mastery over your environment.

The following essay was written by Akane, a student in a U.S. developmental writing course. The assignment was to write about how you learned English. Akane's experiences typify those of many Generation 1.5 students. She was introduced to English before she left her native Japan but did not have a strong command of it when she arrived in the United States. When she writes about how she eventually learned English, she never mentions formal schooling. Instead, she focuses on her opportunities for contact with English-speaking friends, in her case through marching band. She also acknowledges that she still has problems with using English to study.

As you read the essay, consider how Akane's choice of words and expressions relates to her identity. She uses academic vocabulary like *denizen* and *digested* inappropriately and also includes chunks of language more common to spoken English than written, such as *just from the fact, drove me crazy, came up to me,* and *do not have a problem with*. If you were conferencing with Akane, which, if any, of these words and expressions would you try to discuss with her?

In Japan, Language of English is not a completely foreign language. There are many denizens from English. Therefore, English is not like Spanish which very a few Japanese people know how does the Spanish sounds like. Also all Japanese students from middle high school begin to learn how to speak, read, and write in English in school.

I came to the United States when I was 14 years old. Even though I knew how English sounds like or could speak a little bit of English, my views towards English changed a lot with a whole different situation. Before I moved here, I thought I would be able to speak English just from the fact to live in the United States. However, this idea was way too wrong. Everyone was speaking English around me and I could not understand any of the words they were speaking. It drove me crazy that all the people around me were speaking in the *language I could not understand. There was nobody who came up to me to speak with me. However, I could not do anything because I did not know how to speak with them. My life changed a lot by moving to the United States. I was a parson who never became alone. I was always with my friends and was chatting with them all the time. But since I came to the United States, I did not have anyone to talk to or be with for a while. It was really bitter experience for me to deal with; especially I was at age, which was really sensitive time of human's life.*

My turning point was to join the Marching Band in High School. I joined to the Marching Band to make friends, not that I wanted to play instruments. It was really successful. I made many friends in Marching Band and learned how to speak English from them. Although I hated being in Marching Band, I enjoyed spending time with my friends in Marching Band. It was amazing how quickly I digested the language of English. I still have problems with English that are used for studying, but I do not have any problem with talking to English speaker. I do not know how it happened to me. However, one thing for sure is making English speaking friends and having fun with them is always good to learn English.

Tutoring / Teaching Tip

It can be helpful to discuss with students the role of writing in their academic careers as well as their personal lives. Many research studies have shown that motivation has a lot to do with how successful someone is at learning a language. If students see writing as something they do just to impress or satisfy a teacher, then they may be less motivated than if they view writing as a teacher itself. For students who will probably always be less than confident about their linguistic "correctness," it's also important to explode the myth that "good" writing means the absence of error. So, don't be afraid to discuss big picture issues related to an assignment—let the student get his or her beliefs out in the open. Make it clear that it is the ideas that really count.

Varieties of English

Another useful variable for understanding why students write the way they do pertains to the status of English in their native culture or country. Depending on your cultural background and experiences, this passage from an article in an online newspaper in Calcutta, India, may seem to be: (a) a sophisticated treatment of a potentially contentious issue, (b) an "oddly" worded statement, or (c) an example of what happens when a piece of writing is not properly edited.

> *All India Council For Technical Education seems all set for a change. The statutory body was set up in 1987, with a view to proper planning and coordinated development of the technical education system throughout the country, promotion of qualitative improvement of such education in relation to the planned quantitative growth and the regulation and proper maintenance of norms and standards in the technical education system and related matters. So far AICTE has been looked at as a monitoring agency. Its main function, according to common perception, was to control the mushroom growth of engineering colleges and to grant the continuity of colleges.*
>
> *Consequently AICTE is considered to be a dispensable evil by many. Bogged down by court cases and pressure from politicians to not take drastic measures against errant outfits, it's been tough going for the AICTE. Its stability was also somewhat doubtful, given the structure of the organisation depended heavily on officers on deputation. However, despite the problems, AICTE has been doing its bit as a monitoring agency.*
>
> Gautam Banerjea, downloaded from www.thestatesman.net on Oct. 1, 2003.

When I read this passage, I feel that the second sentence *(The statutory body . . .)* is too long for me to really understand. I'm also somewhat confused by the verb tenses in the first paragraph that go from present *(seems)* to past *(was)* back to present *(has been)* and then back to past *(was)*. Finally, I have to write *given ˄the structure of the organisation depended*, and I don't know what *on deputation* means.

> THAT

  You may experience similar reactions to this next piece as well, which was taken from an online newspaper in Lagos, Nigeria.

> *Within one year, a university established by Cross River State government has become a headache for Governor Donald Duke.*
>
>   *When several years ago, the government of Cross River State mooted the idea of establishing its own university, top academics from the state were part of the most vociferous critics of the move. The grouse of those opposed to the establishment of the University of Technology (CRUTECH) stemmed from government's decision to merge the four campuses of the state's various schools to form the university. The schools include The Polytechnic, Calabar; College of Education, Akamkpa; IBB College of Agriculture, Obubra and the new campus of Ogoja. To these antagonists, a fresh school must be built to raise a university. They were also skeptical of the state's ability to fund the new ivory tower. But against all odds, Governor Donald Duke made up his mind, went ahead and blazed the trail by creating the university.*
>
> George Onah, downloaded from www.vanguardngr.com on October 1, 2003.

With this piece I am struck by the use of rare, seemingly obtuse terms like *moot* and *grouse* alongside what to me are idiomatic expressions such as *against all odds* and *blaze the trail*. The reference to the state's authority as *government* instead of *the government* also takes some getting used to.

I do not know anything about the authors of these two articles, but from what I know about the linguistic history of India and Nigeria, I can guess that both authors consider themselves to be native speakers of English—and probably one or two other languages as well. Moreover they would be offended if I suggested they needed help with ESL issues. At the very least they have probably read, written, spoken, and listened in English since the start of their formal schooling. As former British colonies where a number of ethnic and linguistic communities were united under a single political administration, both India and Nigeria recognize English as an official language. Like many countries around the world English serves as a **lingua franca** in part because it does not necessarily privilege one indigenous linguistic group over another. It is an "outside" language for everyone.

What these two texts illustrate, however, is how much of our daily use of English is controlled by locally defined conventions. Odds are that if I asked the authors of these pieces to reread their articles they would not notice any of the irregularities that I notice. They are using English in a way that is totally acceptable to their local community. In the English that I learned in the United States, *moot* is most commonly used as an adjective (e.g., *moot point*), but the Nigerian passage suggests that the verb usage (i.e., *to discuss*) may be more frequent in other places. Likewise phrases such as *on deputation* may be as common in India as *in house* is in the United States. Local conventions may even lead to differences in principles for constructing discourse, like the American English mandate to maintain tense continuity.

The notion that English is spoken in different ways in different places is probably not new to you. Jokes about British English or Southern English or Canadian abound. What may be new, however, is the extent to which English is used for everyday communication outside of the United States, Canada, Britain, and Australia. It may be used as a general lingua franca, often as a residue of a colonial past like in Nigeria, Kenya, and India. It may be used as a way of laying pretense to a cosmopolitan upbringing, of demonstrating and maintaining social prestige. It may also be used primarily in academic settings as the language of instruction in fields where the majority of the textbooks are published in English (e.g., medicine). On the other hand, its use may be limited mainly to interactions with tourists, which means that it is rarely used between locals.

The degree to which a local variety differs from varieties in other communities will often depend on the social and/or political independence of the community using it as well as the historical influences that led to it being used in this location in the first place. What is important to realize, however, is that these world Englishes are not deviant or unstructured. When any community adopts a language for certain social purposes or settings, it sets in motion a process of normalization. That process includes the identification of common terms of reference (e.g., *officers on deputation*), the creation of patterns for how words can be strung together (e.g., acceptability of omitting *that* in *given the structure . . . depended*), and even the setting of limits on sentence and paragraph length.

What happens, though, when students with those norms come to you for help with their writing? The first step is to realize that, in contrast to English language learners, these students do not have developing grammars; they have more or less fixed grammars. That means that terms like *right* and *wrong* are not applicable. Instead we can say *that's not a term I've heard a lot, and some people may not understand what you mean.* Because these are issues of convention arising from fixed-state grammars, though, be prepared that these issues may be even more impervious to change. The more explicit you can be about what marks a construction as "different" for you, the more helpful it will be for the students. Is it a problem regarding the label used to refer to an entity; is it a rule for what can follow a verb—for example, in

U.S. English we *run up* to an event such as an election and we must *give something* (we cannot just *give*)—or is it the degree of embedded clauses? Whatever the issue, remember that the choice to change must be the student's. The student may not want to change what he or she considers part of his or her voice or national identity.

Why Students Do and Do Not Want to Learn to Write

The final generalization about ESL writers pertains to their motivation for learning to write. This is a generalization that cuts across all the groups previously discussed—international students, Generation 1.5 students, and speakers of world Englishes. For any one of these groups, studying in an English-medium environment represents a challenge. They have either chosen or been forced to choose studying in a language and an academic culture that they do not consider their own. The mere fact that they have taken that challenge says something about them and their motivations. They are less likely to see college as a way of putting off tough decisions about the future or as a chance to party before hitting the "real" world. College and their English-mediated education represent an opportunity to advance. As such, they are more likely to be forward looking.

Most students respond well when a teacher can show them that an assignment will be useful for their future. This is especially true for many ESL students. Their priority is not learning for learning's sake but learning as a means to an end. Thus to the extent that you can help them see connections between a present assignment and future responsibilities, you may be able to positively affect their motivation. If you can get them to brainstorm the kinds of writing assignments they may have in the future, then you may make learning to write even more meaningful to them. If you are an instructor, then you have an even greater opportunity to help by designing assignments that require them to research their fields or simulate a writing task from their field. Also, do not be afraid to ask students why they are doing a particular assign-ment. Many may cite a course requirement, but challenge them further to think about what they are learning from doing it. In short, empower them with the tools necessary to see their educa-tion in its long-term context. The more relevant you can make what you are teaching to their futures, the more likely they are to want to hear what you have to say and the more likely they are to profit from their interaction with you.

3

Understanding the Assignment: Purpose, Conventions, and Preferences

Don't Assume: The Situatedness of American Academics

- "Choose one of the texts from our supplemental reading list and write a book report about it."
- "All work should follow the guidelines of the APA Handbook."
- "Choose one or more of the texts we've been reading this semester and write a critical analysis of the author's use of. . . ."
- "Papers should be at least five typed, double-spaced pages long."
- "Write a paper about the lingering effects in Latin America of the encomienda system during the Spanish colonial period. In your response, be sure to think analytically."
- In a coherent paper, discuss your opinion of White's argument regarding. . . ."

It should be fairly obvious that these sentences were lifted from academic writing assignments. They reference course features (reading lists, the *encomienda* system), production guidelines (double-spaced, APA Handbook), and academic buzzwords (*critical, analytically*) in the context of a writing task. What may not be as obvious is that hidden within these sentences are several culturally bound concepts. What is the difference between a book report and a critical analysis? If the instructions say *at least five pages long,* does that mean I should aim for five and a half pages, seven pages, or fifteen pages? What is APA, and more important, which of the *guidelines* are really important? Does *your response* mean my feelings? These are not specifically language issues, but whether you can even begin to answer them may depend a lot on how much of your previous education took place in the United States.

In the United States, learning to write usually starts with kindergarteners or first graders writing descriptions and accounts of their immediate world and experiences—"my dad," "our class trip to the zoo," or "what we did for Thanksgiving." Building on children's love of storybooks and fantasy, creative genres such as stories and poems are soon introduced as a tool for building engagement in writing. Somewhere around the third or fourth grade, however, standardized writing tests appear on the scene, and students start working on their abilities with narrative and descriptive language into the paradigmatic five-paragraph essay— a form that will dominate their assigned writing through at least the end of high school.

The five-paragraph essay represents a culturally approved archetype for structuring and expressing an argument. Frequently it is taught as a formula: an introductory paragraph that ends with a thesis statement, three body paragraphs—each of which develops an aspect of the thesis—and a conclusion that emphasizes what has been said in the paper. It is more than just a structural template, however. It is a **genre,** meaning that it is associated with conventions for style and form, generates conceptions of likely audiences, and persists because it has name recognition. With respect to style, students learn that for a good five-paragraph essay they should slip their beliefs into sentences written with the third-person instead of first (*X is surprising because* Y instead of *I was surprised that* X). They also learn to combine thoughts using complex sentences with dependent clauses and lots of adjectives. With respect to form, they begin thinking of three points to make about any topic and the need to make a clear distinction between points and supporting material using phrases like *for example*. Finally, they learn that they should use factual information and authoritative quotations rather than emotional pleas to convince their audiences.

I am not trying to say that all academic writing in the United States is a five-paragraph essay, but rather that it is the principle vehicle through which U.S. school children learn how to write for school. Depending on the classes they take in high school, they may also enter the university with some knowledge of a research paper, a lab report, a journalistic news story, a book report (a.k.a. a plot summary), and creative fiction or poetry. Teachers often teach these genres, however, by pointing out how they are different from the essay. Thus, if U.S. students have had experience with these other types of writing, odds are they will have an even keener awareness of the distinguishing features of the five-paragraph essay and its cultural defaults.

For students from other educational systems, the whole notion of assigned writing may be different. In the United States, assignments tend to emphasize the writer's ability to analyze or develop an argument; as such they are open-ended, with no right answer. In settings where most classes are large lecture sections, instructors would have to go without sleep for a week in order to grade assignments where every response is different. In order for work to be efficiently graded, assignments need to pose a problem that can be answered by a careful reading of a textbook or a review of lecture notes. Assignments may also be shorter in length, requiring a few sentences or a paragraph at most. In such writing, students have to identify appropriate and sufficient content and command of the linguistic conventions for formal expression, but they do not have to worry as much about encoding a novel argument into a thesis statement or carrying on a dialogue with an imaginary reader in order to make themselves sound convincing.

Alternatively, most of a student's writing may have been in the context of timed exams. Although exam questions often seem like paper prompts, using words like *compare* and *analyze*, the contexts differ in significant ways. With timed writing, there is no chance to engage in a writing "process." What goes on the paper stays on the paper with only minor editing. Because there has been little chance for revision, exams are generally graded for content more than presentation. Grammatical missteps, lack of paragraphing, occasional non sequiturs, and even failures to cite sources can all be overlooked. There is also a clear assumption with an exam that the grader is the audience. Therefore, it is acceptable to make references to *as we discussed in class* or *what you showed us*. In U.S. academic papers, however, we generally expect students to write for a generic academic reader who has not even read the assignment, and we expect at least minimal attention to format and mechanics.

So what does all this mean if you are working with a student? It is generally accepted practice to ask all students to explain the assignment they want help on. With ESL students especially, however, you may need to probe their understanding more deeply. For example, consider the directions for a writing assignment I have given undergraduate students in an introductory linguistics class I teach:

> Answer ONE of the following questions in an essay of approximately five typed pages. Note that for each question, a purpose and audience has been specified. These should be carefully considered when writing. Essays will be graded on the clarity of the argument, the depth of the ideas presented, and the overall writing quality. If you would like to hand in a first draft for comments, you may. First drafts must be handed in by Thursday, November 19. The final copy is due in class on Thursday, December 3.

For many of us, the tendency would be to skim this section of the assignment sheet and focus on the questions that follow and that present specific scenarios warranting a piece of writing (a report to a federal commission, a newspaper editorial, a personal letter, and a news magazine essay). With ESL students, clearly each of the scenarios might require some discussion of the cultural context, but the initial directions may as well.

The initial directions include prescriptions regarding the choice of topic and length, a somewhat unusual highlighting of the need to consider purpose and audience, a vague indication of how the work will be evaluated, and a suggestion that the student engage in a drafting process. Each of these components can require unpacking. The opening sentence calls the paper an essay, yet describes it *as an answer to a question*, which may sound more like a response to a timed exam if that is what you are used to writing. The references to purpose and audience are actually indicators that the student should pretend to be writing something other than a class assignment, a license that students who have not written creatively in school before may not recognize. Likewise terms like *argument, depth,* and *overall quality* come from the lexicon of writing teachers and may require explicit discussion of what they mean in concrete terms. Finally, the whole notion of taking a paper through multiple drafts relies on familiarity with the write-revise-edit-publish process as typically taught in U.S. schools. ESL writers may need to know that there is an implied assumption that a *first draft* and *final copy* will be significantly different.

Students for whom the notion of an assigned, out-of-class writing task is new may also benefit from discussing the purpose of the assignment within the context of the course. Encourage a

Tutoring / Teaching Tip

Discussing key terms in an assignment can lead to a fairly abstract conversation, where the student keeps saying *yeah* and *OK* but has no real frame of reference for understanding what you are talking about. One way of avoiding this is to bring in other sample assignments and ask the student to contrast them with the one he or she has been asked to do.

little ethnographic digging on their part. For example, what does the syllabus say about course learning objectives? Does it mention written communication and, if so, what characteristics of writing are valued? Many syllabi include references to critical thinking. Ask the student what this term means, and if he or she expresses confusion, suggest an Internet search. A search for "Bloom's taxonomy," which categorizes assignment objectives according to the level of abstraction needed to complete the assignment, may prove useful here as well. Finally, in courses with multiple writing assignments, ask the students to consider the relation between the different assignments. Do they all seem to be the same type of writing, or is there a pattern to what the instructors are asking for? Seeing the current paper described as a short paper in comparison to the end-of-term research paper provides a useful context for questions about length and expectations for outside sources. Style guides, such as the *MLA Handbook* and *APA Style Manual*, can be another useful resource when researching assignments. In addition to prescriptive details about bibliographic format and margin size, most style guides also discuss what constitutes good writing in the disciplines that use them.

One final scenario to consider is when the instructor has provided only minimal information regarding expectations for the writing assignment and/or the function of writing in the class. Maybe the instructor has simply told the students verbally to choose a book from a prescribed list and write a two-page summary. This is a fairly generic example, and you probably could just tell the student what you think the instructor wants. For ESL writers, however, it may be more helpful to begin by asking them to identify questions about the assignment. They may have questions about how to start, whether and how much they should quote from the book, and how to refer to the book in the paper. They probably have not thought about why they are being asked to do this, or what are the qualities of a good summary. Work with them to write the questions and impose some organization on them. If there is time, encourage them to use the questions as a starting point for an office hour visit to the instructor. If there is no time, provide your own perspective, but encourage them to ask some other people as well. This may seem a cumbersome approach to communicating the implicit expectations of an assignment, but remember that what you are really doing is preparing them for the next culturally laden, one-sentence assignment description.

Using Sources: Idea Ownership and Credibility

One of the most important sets of conventions related to academic writing assignments covers the use and misuse of sources. At many universities, these conventions are expressed at least superficially in explicit policies requiring the proper documentation of source materials along with a list of punishments for violating them. ESL students must understand these policies and be encouraged to take them seriously. Unfortunately, it is not unusual to spend more time telling students what they should not do than what they should do.

Explanations of citation and plagiarism generally frame the discussion in terms of economic and moral ownership. Authors own the ideas they express in writing as well as the phrasings that they create to express those ideas. Just as inventors may patent their creations, authors (or their publishers) may copyright their publications and then sell the right to reproduce them. If the material a student wants to use is sufficiently limited, he or she can reproduce it without first seeking permission, but he or she must still acknowledge the original owner according to accepted conventions for citation (e.g., MLA, APA, *Chicago*). Failure to do so is considered to be "stealing.".

Over the years, I have received many student papers where after a somewhat awkward introductory paragraph with occasional grammar issues, I would run into several eloquent sentences written with a voice of complete authority, and I would know that I had a problem. I would also know I had a problem when I received papers with two or even three pages of a four-page paper enclosed in quotation marks. Then there are the cases of three different students using the same adjective + noun + prepositional phrase or the paper with the strange alternation between first and third person subjects at each paragraph boundary. The warning signs are many, but in each instance I would know that I had to talk to the student and explain the ethics of citation and plagiarism. Unfortunately, too often I have probably resorted to the explanation about the ownership of ideas and essentially accused my students of thievery without considering their motivations.

With ESL students especially, it is important to start with the issue of why they did what they did. But we have to be careful how we ask the question. If we frame the discussion in terms of ownership, then the question is, "Why didn't you cite sources for borrowed material?" Usually students answer this somewhat disingenuously as, "I didn't know I was supposed to" or "I thought it was OK as long as I listed them in my bibliography." I have usually answered with, "Well, you were supposed to know better." In no time, I am mad, they are mad, and no one has learned anything from the experience except that the other cannot be trusted.

If we reframe the question, however, as "Why did you want to use this material here?" then we may get a more interesting set of responses to work with. We may hear claims about how important an idea seemed or explanations about past writing experiences where the best grades went to the people who could reproduce the most information from the textbook. Alternatively, we may listen to students express fears about twisting an author's intent if they changed the wording or simply how frustrated they are with their inability to express themselves. (In truth, the students may not have enough vocabulary to rephrase the original.) You may also find out about some of their language learning strategies such as writing whole phrases or committing passages to memory in order to learn the rhythms of the language. You may even get a lesson on academic writing in other educational settings and how much students are expected to defer to experts.

None of these answers absolves a student of having failed to cite a source properly or remove the stigma associated with excessive quotation, but they open the door to discussing how and why we rely on sources in academic writing, which needs to be a shared understanding before talking about citation formats. The traditional explanation is that sources provide support for our ideas. Sometimes support comes in the form of factual data. It may also provide a developed argument or explanation for a claim we have made. Alternately, it may be an opinion from a figure with enough authority to command respect. Regardless of the content of the source material, students need to understand the expectation that it will serve a supporting role in what they write. Its primary function is to give credibility to their thoughts, evaluations, and arguments. When we frame the use of sources as a way of achieving credibility, students may realize that acknowledging as many authors as possible is to their advantage. Relying on others is not stealing; it is a good thing as long as they do it properly.

We still have to look out for the students who have not developed an argument to support or who have totally relied on someone else's, but we can get at these issues by asking them to provide a verbal outline or summary of their work. When a student seems unable to break free from something they have read and simply strings together details from different works, try asking him or her to summarize one work at a time (in as few a words as possible). After the summary, ask opinion questions about the work and how the student thinks it relates to the topic. What you are doing here is teasing out the framework that has to be there for the source material to support.

Once we have developed an understanding of how citation strengthens a paper, all that remains is format. There are at least three different situations where attribution is required: (1) the use of another's exact words (quotation), (2) the use of the gist of an author's sentences but not the exact words (paraphrase), and (3) a capsulation of another's work at the level of an argument (summary). Unfortunately, many teachers assume that how to quote is obvious and then subsume the second and third situations into one discussion about how to paraphrase. Citing legalistic rules about how many words can be repeated from an original source, these teachers create exercises in thesaurus use and rephrasing.

Choosing the appropriate form, however, requires more than knowledge of how to use quotation marks and a thesaurus.

Incorporating source material should begin with an understanding of the scope of what is to be incorporated. Is the material a developed argument or thematic element expressed across multiple sentences, paragraphs, or even sections of a work? Or, is it drawn from a single location in the text? If it is drawn from multiple sections, then its inclusion constitutes a summary. Often summaries are incorporated into a text as a single sentence using the author's name plus verbs such as *argues, believes, describes,* or *concludes.* An extended summary may describe an argument with more detail using a frame such as *AUTHOR + states three reasons why . . .* or the more narrative *AUTHOR begins by . . . then.*

If the material is drawn from a single location, then the writer needs to decide whether to quote or paraphrase. In advanced academic writing, quotations of single or multiple sentences are generally reserved for effect. They may use language that is especially eloquent, strong, or be an opinionated statement from someone whose opinion matters. If quoting multiple sentences, there is a fine art to deciding where to begin and where to end the quote. Sometimes, a writer will also quote a short phrase that indicates how another author labeled something or just the evaluative portion of a source sentence. Paraphrasing, on the other hand, serves as a default for the inclusion of more factual information that is not general knowledge.

Tutoring / Teaching Tip

Find an article in an academic journal related to the student's field and ask the student to analyze a paragraph with multiple citations. Ask the student to distinguish between content created by the author and content that relates to something in the sources being cited. Try to find an instance where a single sentence contains multiple citations, and ask the student why the author would have done that and what impression that gives of the author. You can also use the article to find examples of quotations, paraphrases, and summaries. Explore issues such as the relative proportion of each, where they occur in the text, and how they are incorporated into sentence structures.

This list of functions is not exhaustive, but it should open up some ideas for issues you can explore with a student. It is important to remember also that conventions differ from one academic discipline to another about issues such as whether to incorporate an author's name into the sentence or put it in parentheses at the end of the sentence and the appropriate length for quotations. The bottom line, however, is to help the student develop a functional understanding of when and how to use source material rather than trapping the student in a purely formal set of dos and don'ts.

Personal Expression and Voice

The hidden assumptions and values that academic readers bring to assigned writing cover both formal characteristics and functional components. One of the most intangible assumptions, however, relates to the need for voice—a need to make even an objective text carry a stamp of personal expression. Composition teachers often explicitly encourage students to "find their voice," while faculty assigning writing in the disciplines may phrase it as wanting to know "your thoughts and ideas." From their perspective, voice provides insight into the student's thinking and ability to control the message communicated by the text. For students from other cultures, however, it may come across as pressure to reveal a private side or to pretend to be authorities when they feel they should be apprentices.

Cultural anthropologists root this potential conflict in a society's preference for collective consensus versus individual freedom. For our purposes, it probably relates more to the way students are taught to write than their actual products. In some composition classes, teachers encourage students to find ideas through techniques such as freewriting, journaling, or reaction papers. They want students to discover their own ideas before becoming immersed in someone else's through close readings or topic research. If students have been taught to begin writing by listening to what their teachers and experienced scholars have said about a topic, then this approach may seem backward or even invasive. Not all ESL students come from collectivist cultures and even some who do may not resist such techniques, but you should be aware of the potential conflict if you are advising students how to begin working on an assignment.

Probably the more difficult issue is explaining to students what we mean by voice and how we demonstrate it in writing. In terms of the devices that signal its presence, voice is similar to style and tone. All three are signaled by the use across a text of words, grammatical patterns, and sentence structures that connote a consistent affective message. **Style** usually describes how the language of a text associates it with a category of texts. When I talk about *academic style*, I am using the sound of a text to group it with other texts written in educational settings; I am also making the implicit claim that it sounds different from "informal" letters or "romantic" novels. **Tone** implies a more transient, but still generally recognizable affective message. Often used to describe a passage as opposed to a whole text, a writer's tone can be at times "playful," "arrogant," or "dark." **Voice**, on the other hand, implies an author's ability to personalize his or her writing, to somehow distinguish it from other authors' texts. It may be characteristic language that cuts across all the author's writing—for example, a predilection for rhetorical questions or emotive adjectives. More commonly, however, it refers to an author's ability to make personal opinions and beliefs felt in his or her text.

A text with voice indicates that an author in fact holds a perspective of the entity or event being described. A text without voice may appear confused, leaving the reader guessing what the author really thought. Alternatively, and this is often the case with ESL students, it may use language that is generic or that does not have strong connotations. This type of writing often prompts teachers to write, *But what do you think?* in the margin. Ironically though, the same teacher may comment *unnecessary* if the student begins too many sentences with *I think* or *it seems to me* because voice is also usually assumed to involve more subtle techniques.

In trying to explain voice to a student, there are two parts to keep in mind: the message and the forms used to convey the message. The message is the author's perspective. In this book, for example, I am trying to craft a voice that conveys a number of messages including that I know what I am talking about, I am empathetic with the needs of writing teachers and consultants, and I respect the difficulties faced by ESL writers. Alternatively, I could have chosen to feel that teachers are generally misguided in their approaches and that my job was to show them where they are wrong or that I need the help of experts to give my book credibility. If you are trying to get a handle on what voice is, think about how this book and even this particular paragraph would have needed to be different if I had adopted these other perspectives.

The answers could probably fill a book of their own, so I am going to hit on just a few devices that we use for conveying our perspective:

- **Modals:** Broadly speaking, modals function like helping verbs and indicate whether the author believes an action to be a possibility (*can, could, may, might*), a necessity (*must, might, have to, should, had better*), or a future likelihood (*be going to, will, would*). Because I am wary of generalizing about second language writers, you will notice, for example, that many of the claims I make in this book use possibility modals.
- **Stance adverbials:** These are words (*strangely, unfortunately, certainly*) and expressions (*without doubt, in an unusual move*) that convey the author's opinion about the information in the rest of the sentence. They are sometimes set apart from the sentence either at the beginning or inside commas.
- **Value-laden words:** Many—but not all—words invoke positive or negative connotations. Compare, for example, the meaning conveyed by *a rash judgment, a quick judgment,* and *a speedy judgment*. All refer to the limited amount of

time necessary to render the judgment, but you could probably also infer whether I thought that was good or bad by which one I chose to use.

- **Person:** Handbooks sometimes advise students to avoid using first person (*I*, *me*, *my*, *we*, *our*) or second person (*you*, *your*) in academic writing. Composition teachers then come back and say, "Well, it depends." If we use first and second person, it is usually because we want the text to sound as if it were part of a dialogue or discussion. It conveys the message that we want our reader to feel that we are personally involved with their issues. The use of first person alone, on the other hand, is often associated with expressions such as *I believe* or *from my perspective*, which explicitly signal the author's voice.

This list is intended to suggest high-frequency aspects of language to which you could pay specific attention when discussing either the student's work or an example passage. Use it as a starting point for helping students to recognize voice in writing. Start with questions such as, "What do you want this phrase to tell me about your opinion?" or "Why do you think the author uses *might* here?" Then follow up by asking the student to find other examples that convey the same message. When students are struggling to interpret a passage, they are looking for explanations about meaning and they are more likely to remember the answer than if it is an example on a handout.

The messages that constitute an author's voice generally derive from the connotations of words and grammatical patterns, not from an application of dictionary definitions or handbook explanations. ESL students may know that *rash* means "quick," but it is less likely they will know that it is frequently used negatively. Sometimes they will figure this out through repeated exposure, but it is often helpful to make them realize that such information really should be part of their mental associations for the word. Understanding the expectations of assigned writing in a new academic culture involves consciousness-raising. Even more than explicit guidelines, ESL students need to know the questions they should be asking. The degree to which they feel comfortable using personally expressive language in an assignment must ultimately be their choice, but it should be a choice.

The assumption of much of this discussion has been that you are working with students who do not know what we mean by voice. This paper was written by an Arab student reacting to an article about environmental crises in the Middle East. There are many ways that the essay could be improved, but it also provides several good examples of devices that create voice. Think how you might use it to show a student you are working with what voice is.

I felt a sense of anger while reading the article. This is because many countries in the Mediterranean are not taking the issue seriously. There are many negative things that are to happen only years away from now but none are taken into consideration.

First of all, the great increase of population that is expected by 2025 means denser urban cities which could mean more diseases and chaos at the same time that there would be less places for people to reside and not enough services to meet the demand of and increasingly growing population.

The problem extends to the fact that this huge population would probably require more power plants to produce electricity. This leads to increase in pollution. The environment in the Mediterranean is desperate for a rest but it seems that things will only keep on getting worse!

In addition to that, the fresh water deficiency that is expected to happen in the Mediterranean could cause many problems. This is because people in that area are already dying from thirst and not enough water means death rate will continue to thrive.

Moreover, power plants could not provide the enough energy to meet the demand of this huge population. Natural resources are running into scarcity. People are going to have to return to primitive life styles in serving themselves.

We are also clearly aware about how road traffic is creating a problem in the Mediterranean. With the increase of population density, traffic is going to continue to increase. This results in more pollution and more chaos.

With more population, disposal wastes are going to increase at the shores of the Mediterranean. Huge amounts of wastes are expected to be dumped at these shores by 2025. This creates more pollution and a ruined environment.

Desertification is also creating a big problem in the Mediterranean. This is due to the fact of urbanization and lack of water resources. It is going to create problems such as food and income shortages due to less fertile lands.

All of these problems are creating a huge threat towards the environment in that area. We did notice some quite noticeable changes such as the use of the natural gas vehicles in Egypt and a couple of agreements but this is not enough. The case has to be taken more seriously as people's lives and major ecosystems are endangered.

All of these actions together created the sense of anger within me. Thinking of what has happened and what is to happen convinces us that we are desperate for a change. Looking back at what was done to treat the problem evolves even more anger on how careless societies can be towards the good being of their own environments.

We need to change every single person's mentality towards their environment. Perhaps, the easiest ways to do that is to educate people. Students should learn the importance of the issues through their school programs. Colleges should start dense campaigns in public to aware people of those dangers.

Another thing that could be done to limit these threats is by implementing heavy taxes on all of those companies or individuals who abuse the environment. This could be done at the minor scale such as punishing those who ruin the environment by

littering or smoking in non-smoking areas for example. Actions taken at the larger scale create a big change as well. Laws should severely restrict the polluting of the environment by factories, their products, or buildings.

One thing we can tell people to convince them is to tell them that there is still hope. This could encourage people and drive them to create a change!

Tutoring / Teaching Tip

Review the editorial section of a Sunday newspaper, which often features two articles with contrasting viewpoints on a topic. Look for examples of the devices listed here as a starting point for a discussion of the authors' views of the topic and the relationship they wish to establish with the reader.

Where to Stick It: Organizational Strategies

Organization is a hot topic when it comes to writing. Many grading rubrics explicitly target organization along with content and grammar. Professors often simply write *organization* as a comment in red on papers. Some composition classes are even structured around practicing specific organizational patterns such as compare and contrast, problem and solution, and cause and effect. In Chapter 1, however, I claimed that it is very hard not to organize a piece of writing. I said this because I don't believe that lack of organization is a big problem for student writers; I think the issue more often is an ineffective or misleading organization for a given purpose or audience.

Admittedly, the distinction I am making here is a subtle one. But if an essay were truly unorganized, then our task would be to help students create structure where none exists, to teach them patterns that they can use to locate information for a reader. Many writing handbooks take this approach when they teach organizational patterns as part of a chapter on drafting or planning. They may share pre-formed structures such as this one for a paragraph in an expository essay:

- Major Claim
  - Supporting Point 1
    - Example of Supporting Point 1
  - Supporting Point 2
    - Example of Supporting Point 2
- Restatement of Claim

Or, they may advocate beginning a persuasive essay by listing the counterarguments and then pointing out the problems with them as a way of setting up the actual argument.

If we are tutoring, however, we are usually not working with students who come to us with nothing. They may have a page of notes, an outline, or even a completed draft. If we are a teacher planning a writing course, it is still questionable whether we should spend a lot of time on generic organizational structures. As writing tutors and teachers, I think we can be more helpful if we work with students to realize the structure that they have in place (i.e., start with what they know) and then lead them to evaluate its effectiveness.

Consider this paragraph that Juan wrote as part of an informative research paper on careers in nanotechnology. Juan had identified a number of different fields with potential applications in nanotechnology and had written one paragraph about each. He headed this paragraph Electrical and Electronics Engineers:

[1] James D. Meindl is an electrical and computer engineering professor who is involved in nanotechnology research. He predicts that engineers will use nanotechnology to shrink today's transistors by a factor of 10, providing terascale integration chips that contain more than a trillion transistors (Rupley, 2001). [2] Currently, electrical and electronics engineers are working on the development of new computer chips that will increase data storage capacity 1000 times greater. [3] Electrical and electronics engineers design, develop, test, and supervise the manufacture of electrical and electronic equipment. In addition, they design new products, develop maintenance schedules, test equipment, solve operating problems, and estimate the time and cost of engineering projects. Electronic and electrical engineers are employed in scientific research, government agencies, and manufacturers of computers and electronic products and machinery. [4] According to a 2003 salary survey by the National Association of Colleges and Employers, bachelor's degree candidates in electrical and electronics engineering received starting offers averaging $49,794 a year, master's degree candidates averaged $64,556, and Ph.D. candidates averaged $74,283 (U.S. Department of Labor, 2004–05).

When I read this paragraph, my first reaction is, Who is James Meindl and why should I care? I am stuck at the very beginning. As I read further, I realize that he wants to say that electrical engineering is one field where people can do research that involves nanotechnology—as exemplified by Meindl. But then I feel like the information about what electrical engineers do generally and their salary range is tacked on rather than being central to what Juan wants to explain. In short, the information is not presented in a way that makes sense to me.

Discussing Organization

So how could I help Juan improve this paragraph and the paper overall? I suppose I could give him a handout on general to specific organizational patterns and talk about the hourglass structure of some example paragraphs that start with a broad claim and then move to a specific instance before moving back to a statement that gets the reader to think at the general level again. My problem with this approach is that it ignores what Juan was trying to do and doesn't explain why I have problems with his paragraph. It also promotes the notion that good writing is little more than getting the formula right.

The first step in discussing organization of a paper that has already been written is to invoke a level of abstraction. We need to identify component parts and come up with labels for them. I identified four sections in Juan's paragraph, which I marked with bracketed numbers:

1. Example of an electrical engineer doing nanotechnology research
2. Specific description of nanotechnology research that electrical engineers do
3. General description of what electrical engineers do
4. Salary prospects for electrical engineers

Note that the first, second, and fourth sections correspond to single sentences but the third encompasses three sentences. If I were discussing the organization of a whole paper, my sections might or might not be single paragraphs. Sentences and paragraphs chunk language into units that a reader can mentally process. Sometimes those units correspond to content chunks; sometimes they correspond to a physical processing limit. Note also, that for labels, I combined functional (i.e., description, example) and relational (i.e., general/specific) terms because I wanted to capture not only what the parts do but also how they fit in with what is before and after. If I were talking about a more persuasive piece of writing I might be using terms like *claim, support, set up,* or *conclude.*

Identifying and labeling sections of a text makes it possible to move to the next step: discussing the *effect* in *effectiveness.* Before I move into how his paragraph affected me, though, it would probably be best to ask Juan why he ordered the sections the way he did. Why did he start with the specific example? He might reveal that he wanted to begin by grabbing the reader's attention and that he thought a real person was more interesting than a description of electrical engineering. At this point, I should realize that he in fact had an organizational strategy, which was to move from more to less interesting. If I am really alert, I might even point out to him that this is the dominant organizational pattern for news stories, which like to start with the number of dead bodies before explaining the background causes of the violence. As the structure for an individual paragraph in a larger text, however, it does not really work for me because it does not give me an incentive to go to the next paragraph. I might suggest, however, that we maintain the goal of inserting something concrete in the first sentence in order to make it interesting.

Now that I have given Juan a chance to explain his original intentions, I need to share with him my experience as a reader. One way of thinking about organization is as how a writer chooses to sequence the reader's experience. Juan's paragraph caused me problems because I started with a section heading, Electrical and Electronics Engineers, in a paper titled Nanotechnology Job Prospects, and so I expected an explanation of how this field was related to career opportunities in nanotechnology. Instead I encountered a person's name. When Meindl was identified as an electrical engineer, I was able to keep going, but I had a nagging question. Then, when the next sentence explained the range of nanotechnology research done by electrical engineers, I went backward to figure out which type Meindl did. I was really not prepared when I got to an explanation of what electrical engineers do, even though the heading (3 experiences earlier) had suggested that this was coming. Instead of propelling me forward, the sequence sent me backward as a reader.

People who are interested in writing as a craft like to map out how a text is structured as a whole and, for them, that map represents the organization of the text. The map may be an outline that sorts ideas hierarchically according to degrees of relevance (i.e., main idea, supporting idea, detail). It may be a schematic flow chart with arrows connecting encapsulated ideas in order to represent a chronological sequence or a logical syllogism. When discussing organization with a student, however, it is important to communicate that such maps are only available to readers in hindsight and only if they care to figure out that the paragraph they just read resembles an hourglass or a set of stairs or a mountain trek.

Most people don't read a text in order to create a graphic representation of it; they read it in order to get to the end. Organization is apparent and effective if their expectations at any point in the text are met by the next point. Juan needs a grand scheme for his paragraph, and although it might not have been clear to you the first time you read it, I think he has one. But his grand scheme needs adjusting because he is trying to meet expectations of interest rather than information. Juan did not fail to organize his text; rather, he misgauged his reader. To work with him on organization, we therefore need to verbalize our thoughts as readers—both

Tutoring / Teaching Tip

One way to help students predict the reader's experience is to ask them to read a text aloud, if possible one with a similar purpose to theirs. Ask them to stop at the end of each sentence or other prescribed points to predict what the writer will say next. If prediction is hard, ask them what questions they have at this point in the text. Last, ask them to do the same with their piece of writing.

the chunks we see in his text and what we expect based on those chunks. We also need to get him into the habit of asking the questions that a reader would ask. Improving organization is a matter of getting into a reader's experience of a text and figuring out what is needed next.

Reader Expectations and Second Language Writers

If organization is a chronological series of choices made by a writer trying to fulfill expectations, then it is important for students to understand the types of expectations that readers may have. This may be particularly difficult, however, for second language writers who do not necessarily share with their readers a common culture or depth of experience with English texts. As previously noted, we can help them simply by verbalizing a reader's thoughts about their work; we also can talk with them about conventions, both the conventions that allow us to associate a text with a particular genre and the conventions that exist for how we achieve rhetorical goals like explanation, narration, and persuasion.

Genres

Genres represent named categories of texts such as lab reports, expository essays, historical novels, and business memos. They serve designated purposes (report, espouse, entertain, summarize) within specific communities (biologists, academics, business professionals), and often the ability to produce a particular genre is a marker of membership in the community. Journalists have to be able to write news stories, and college students have to be able to write an analysis paper or produce an annotated bibliography. Some genres have very rigid and explicitly marked organizational conventions. Published reports of experimental research studies, for example, almost always begin with a literature review followed by method and analysis, results, and discussion sections. For most genres, however, the organizational conventions may not be as readily apparent to students.

In these cases, it is helpful to begin by addressing how we even recognize a text as belonging to a particular genre. The clues that a reader uses include the medium of publication (e.g., academic journal, newspaper, parchment paper, website), formatting devices (e.g., headings, colored ink, varied font sizes), and even the way the text begins (e.g., *The following report suggests . . .*).

Consider these student texts. What genres do you associate them with and why?

[1] In "Repositioning of Citizenship: Emergent Subjects and Spaces for Politics" Saskia Sassen discusses the impact of globalization on the nations and how it affects citizenship and nationalism. Sassen starts by laying out the definition of both citizenship and nationality, showing their relationship, and analyzing the limitation of the definition of citizenship on a single nation. Due to this definition, she defines the social rights of citizens and how citizens interact with their society; as equals and not discriminating between each other. The author then shows which individuals from the public act in the process of developing the political and social systems, whether being "authorized yet not recognized," i.e. housewives, or "unauthorized yet recognized," i.e. illegal immigrants. Furthermore, the author argues against the "nation-based citizenship," the theory claims that a citizen must be limited to one nation; she further interprets how citizens might not be limited to a single nation and discuses the impacts of the theory. Finally, she sums up the article with the most important issue, the creation of the "global city." She criticizes the "global city," discussing the advantages and disadvantages and how as a result that changes the social structure of nations, increasing the confusion and implications of the definition of 'citizenship'.

[2]

Date: 20 January 2009
From: ...
To: Dr. Dudley W. Reynolds
              Associate Teaching Professor of English
Subject: Readability comparison of two similar texts

The purpose of this memo is to contrast the readability of two English texts of the same topic. One of the texts is an encyclopedia entry and the other is from an online source, Wikipedia. Though both articles discuss basically the same topic, the differences in targeted readers give them opposite levels of readability. This memo will analyze the two articles and emphasize on the issues that make an article more readable.

The two texts that are being compared are encyclopedia definitions of the word "Synapse". The main difference between them is that one of them is more readable than the other. Since the topics are the same, it will be easier to find out the key features of a text that make it more readable.

To make the comparison easier to understand I first labeled different sections of the texts based on what I thought the author was trying to do. Then I looked at the common sections and analyzed themes like use of technical terms, organization. When I moved on to sections that are unique to the texts, I began analyzing the assumptions the author made while presenting new material. At the end, I concluded that one of the articles I analyzed seemed more readable to me because it appeared to be written with readers of my knowledge level in mind. . . .

From my analysis I can conclude that the Wikipedia article is more comprehensible to me than the encyclopedia article. Its simple organization of introducing new topics in new paragraph makes it very easy it to read. The text is presented in a way so that context is given before explanation. This helps understanding the article much easier. And lastly, the article cites its sources; hence it will be very easy for me to use parts of the article for future reference. Overall, I would give the Wikipedia article a better readability score.

Without much difficulty you hopefully labeled the first a summary and the second a memo. To arrive at these conclusions, you may have started with the information that they were written by students, which led you to exclude genres such as news stories and novels. Since the first text was only one paragraph long, you may also have figured out that it was not a research paper, lab report, or anything that we would describe as a major writing assignment. When you began reading the first text, you found the title of an article and its author's name in the first sentence. You probably did not need to read any further to guess that it was a summary. If it had been a comparison piece, you would have expected references to more than one article. If it had been a critique, you would have expected a more opinionated statement about the contents of the article. With the second text, the formatting for the specifications of date, author, audience, and subject immediately reveal that this is not a business letter or a book report or an annotated bibliography.

For our purposes here, the expectations these clues invoke for a reader are what is important. Summaries typically serve one of two purposes in academic communities. Students may write them for classes across academic disciplines as a way of demonstrating that they have read a text. They may also be asked to produce them in a writing class as an exercise that prepares them to write longer, more analytic papers such as critiques or research papers. Either way, the summary functions as an abbreviated version of an original source, and faithfulness to the original is tantamount. Therefore, I typically expect a summary to begin with an announcement of what is being summarized followed by a rephrasing of the major point or thesis of the work—in essence, a mini-summary embedded within the longer summary. The rest of the summary should then take me through the source work in an order that is more or less parallel to the original order of presentation as a way of letting me know how the original author developed the work.

Memos, on the other hand, are not usually thought of as academic genres. They belong to professional communities. When we find them in academic settings, they resemble a role play preparing students for post-graduation writing. Part of the simulation, however, is to imagine an audience for whom time is money. This audience expects the first paragraph to provide a succinct statement of the purpose for the memo (e.g., *This memo specifies the new vacation policy*) or the conclusions reached (e.g., *This memo outlines the reasons for recommending purchase of . . .*). This paragraph allows readers to evaluate whether they need to read the whole document. The rest of the memo then typically repeats in an enhanced mode the information in the first paragraph according to an organization set up by that paragraph.

By pointing out typical structures for summaries or memos, it may sound like I am advocating teaching generic patterns for different genres. I am not. In order for students to utilize these patterns in their writing, the patterns have to be motivated. They have to be seen as a way of meeting a reader's needs, and I think they can be best introduced in the context of a discussion about why would a reader pick up your writing and what would they hope to gain from reading it. These questions address reader expectations at the broadest level, but they can also serve as segues into *What will they want to know first? What else will they want to know?* and *How can we prepare them for this realization?* Finally, they can lead to discussions of other texts that share similar purposes and audiences and how they met their readers' expectations.

One question that remains is whether second language writers face special difficulties with genre conventions. Some of the genres that students encounter in a U.S. university are new to them whether they are writing in their first language or their fifth, and the conventions have to be learned from scratch. Other genres, however, such as summaries, research papers, and reaction journals are frequently introduced in high school or even earlier. Since these genres may not be used as heavily in secondary education in other countries, it is possible that second language writers will not have written them before or they may have written something with a similar name but different organizing conventions. Even if they

attended a U.S. high school and were in a language arts class designated for second language learners, then they may have focused
more on mastering the kind of five-paragraph essay necessary for
standardized exams and less on writing a range of genres. These
intercultural differences are further compounded by the fact that
many classroom genres do not exist in published forms and so students do not have a chance to develop a sense for them except
through peer review opportunities. If they have not produced a
genre before or even been exposed to it through reading, then
clearly the conventions for organizing it will be problematic.

In working with second language writers on genre conventions, it is again important not to
assume that you are working
with a blank slate. Discuss with
them parallel forms of writing
that they may have done previously. Ask them how these forms
were developed. Sometimes you
may find that they simply need
encouragement to apply what

> **Tutoring / Teaching Tip**
>
> Since discussing the question *How do you organize summaries in your language?* may be a fairly difficult question for a student to answer, encourage the student to search the Internet for an example text. Let the student then describe the way the example text is developed.

they already know. Other times they may describe a pattern that
strikes you as odd or different. Share your reaction and what you
would expect. In the process you will be building their meta-aware-
ness of writing as a craft and the possibilities they have for shaping
a reader's experience.

Rhetoric

The organizing conventions associated with a genre typically refer
to the placement of named sections (e.g., heading in a memo,
body in a letter, abstract in a research report, executive summary
in a report), the development of a section (e.g., state the purpose
of the memo in the first paragraph), and possibly the use of for-
mulaic sequences (e.g., "These findings suggest . . . " begins a new
section in a research report). There are also conventions, however, associated with what we might term *rhetorical goals* that are

invoked across any number of genres when we want to do things like explain, persuade, or flatter.

The term *rhetoric* entered the English language from Greek. In the Greek city states of the fourth and fifth centuries BCE, the term referred specifically to the craft of argument and the techniques that public speakers could use to convince an audience. Rhetorical study included not only how to organize a discourse, but also how to come up with something to say about a topic and what types of information would be likely to convince an audience. Today rhetoric often refers more broadly to the study of how speakers (and writers) achieve specific purposes.

Of particular relevance to helping students with organization is the Greek and Latin rhetoricians' recognition of fundamental patterns for expanding an issue in order to achieve a goal or purpose. The Greek term for these patterns was *topoi,* and originally they were intended to function as memory crutches—questions and patterns that speakers could rely on once they identified their purpose for speaking to allow them to start as quickly as possible. Discussions of *topoi* and their usefulness varied with time and author, but among other precepts they introduced the notion that we can argue about whether something happened or will happen, whether it is more/less X than Y, and whether it is possible. Other discussions noted that entities with a shared relevance to a particular issue may be treated as parts of a whole or as distinct instances of a class of items. Finally, they suggested using definitions, divisions, comparisons, and classifications to set up the conditions or assumptions necessary for convincing a reader of a position.

Given the considerable influence of classical Greek scholarship on Western education up to the present day, it is not surprising that these patterns identified more than 2,000 years ago in Greek public discourse continue to be used extensively today. Consider this book: It is an argument about what should happen when we tutor or teach second language writers. The chapters describe different parts of a tutoring process (the whole) and use definitions of terms (e.g., **topoi**), divisions of writers into classes (e.g., international and Generation 1.5), comparisons of different texts, and classifications (e.g., types of devices for conveying voice) to convince you that the process being advocated is in fact productive.

Clearly, the Greek *topoi* are not the only influential organizational crutches for English—think about problem and solution, cause and effect, and order of importance, to name a few others. What is important here is to recognize that not only do good writers rely on organizational archetypes to generate text, but readers also use them to form an interpretive frame for a passage as a way of understanding what is going on. The result is a cyclical strengthening of these patterns. You probably use many of them in your writing simply because they are frequent patterns that you have come across in your reading and they are the first thing that comes to your mind. We have to be careful though not to assume that the patterns that have achieved dominance in English are universal or that students learning to write in English resort to them as naturally as you do.

Consider this prompt for an in-class writing assignment in a composition class. The students had been reading articles about citizenship in an era of globalization.

> You have been asked to teach a course next year that will promote good citizenship. Write an essay in which you describe what you would like students to learn from your class. Refer to the articles you have read and also include examples of activities that might help students to achieve the goals you set.

What do you identify as the purpose of a response to this prompt, and what would you think that you need to do in the paper? You probably would focus on the second sentence—which calls on you to make an argument for what will happen in the future (*describe what you would like students to learn from your class*). What strategies come to your mind to achieve this? Do you think of producing a list of three or four qualities of good citizens (division)? Do you decide to focus on a definition of citizenship and then consider ways that a person can be a bad citizen as a way of setting up what a good citizen would be (comparison)? Do you decide on a more inductive approach in which you propose a sequence of readings identifying key elements from each?

You have not been discussing citizenship for the past two weeks and you have not read any of the articles that this class did, but yet you can read this prompt and quickly imagine a way of addressing it. The strategies you are coming up with probably draw heavily on rhetorical conventions. Now consider Rena's response:

> Citizenship is not only having the nationality of a country, it is such an extent as feeling of loyalty and belonging to a county and the human rights of individuals within a country. Individuals' acts are the mirror that reflects the country. So students should learn the exact meaning of citizenship; they should also practice it because they are the power of the coming generation.
>
> By the end of the course, I would like my students to leave with a strong conviction on citizenship. Knowing the right meaning of citizenship as well as applying it to their daily life. Also, understanding the changes of a state that may change the meaning of citizenship as time changes, in the past citizenship was defined or considered as a part of nationality but not any more. And in the future, globalization will define what citizenship is; yet, students should know that human rights and equal treatment will always be a part of citizenship. In order for students to like the subject and enjoy the class, I will encourage them to behave ethically and hold social responsibilities so that they will have responsibilities toward every single thing in the country and avoid what might harm the country. I will also include different activities such as community service and political debates. This will encourage the students to work harder for their country and get to know or participate in the political system.
>
> It is important to have belonging to one nationality as it is important to have loyalty toward one country. In order to have full rights and be treated equally, individuals should show respect and provide service to the state so that, the right meaning of citizenship will be applied to individuals' lives.

There are elements of the strategies previously listed in this response, but it seems to be a mixture. It starts off by defining citizenship through dividing it into two parts: nationality and a feeling of loyalty. Then it introduces the argument that citizenship should be taught because the individual's actions reflect on the country. Learning goals for the course are then listed as developing a "strong" conviction (classification), knowing the difference between old and new definitions (division into classes), seeing human rights and equal treatment as part of citizenship (division of whole into parts), and encouraging social responsibility and ethical behavior (arguing for what should be). Next the activities are divided into community service and political debates. It is not totally clear to me what Rena's strategy for her final paragraph is, but it seems to resort to stating what good citizenship should entail.

In critiquing Rena's paper it is important to remember that it was written in class with little time to revise. I would also continue to argue that it is not unorganized; it progresses from general to specific back to more general and has elements that clearly build on a previous element as marked by the use of *also* and the repetition of future tense verbs in the middle paragraph. But it does not fit into any of the mental categories I have for how to develop a prompt like this; it seems to mix many different strategies without really developing any of them. Rena might have structured her body paragraph around a list of activities that she classified according to their desired outcomes. She might also have stated an overarching goal for the course that she then divided into parts. She might even have compared what she would do in the course to another course as a way of showing how it would have a unique outcome.

It is tempting to wonder if Rena's response reflects conventions from her first language, Arabic. Maybe it does. There have been studies comparing what readers remember from a second language writer's text when they speak the same first language as the writer and when they do not, and often more is remembered when the reader and writer share the same first language. I am not sure, however, that knowing the extent to which Arabic has influenced Rena's writing is really that important. I definitely should not simply classify her as a "bad" writer because I cannot be certain what conscious or subconscious principles she is applying here, but I also should not use native language as an excuse to dismiss the problems I have understanding her message.

What I see in Rena's response is a need for exposure and practice. Much of what I know about how to write a description in English comes from having read many descriptions. Rena does not have the same luxury of time that I have had, however. If she had the chance to rewrite this paper, it might be helpful to provide her with several short descriptions of abstract concepts like humanism or Marxism. Ask her to create a structural map of each text—the kind we said most readers do not create because it has to be done in retrospect. Work together to identify common patterns like describing by breaking into component parts, starting with what something is not, or narrating the evolution of a concept. Once she has identified a pattern, ask her to talk through how she might apply it to a different topic. Finally, when she feels comfortable talking about organizational patterns, ask her to analyze her original paper in the same way. The goal is to expand Rena's repertoire, to give her tools like the Greeks' *topoi* that she can call on quickly when she has to write an in-class essay, structure a research paper on nanotechnology, or brainstorm a product description in a meeting with business colleagues.

Teaching Conventions

I have argued here that reader expectations are based in conventions for the development of specific genres and more broadly construed rhetorical purposes. I have also suggested introducing these conventions in relation to texts that students are trying to produce rather than as generic patterns in the language. Many writing teachers get nervous, however, when we begin to talk about conventions or patterns or even worse models. What they justly fear is teaching students to conform to formulas, to produce writing that is devoid of voice or creativity. I like the term *convention* because it reveals that these are patterns that have developed through usage, not because they are inherently correct. In sharing them with students, however, it is still important to emphasize that they are not rules but aids and that, in fact, some of the most interesting writing succeeds by breaking conventions and surprising the reader.

Expectations for Language: Cohesion and Lexis

Chapter 4 argued that organization entails developing and sequencing content according to language-specific conventions. The result is "thinking," which frequent readers of that language recognize. When I talk about the thinking in a text, I am taking a top-down perspective to reading; I am focused more on the message than what appears on paper. As I stated in Chapter 1, however, with second language writers in particular we must also be bottom-up readers; we cannot assume that once the message is there, the language will fall into place.

Just as readers have expectations about how topics and arguments will be developed, they also have expectations—developed through repeated exposure—about when and how language will be used. We often phrase these expectations simply by saying that writing needs to be "grammatical," a convenient catch-all term for a range of language patterns. If we are trying to explain to an English language learner why a sentence "doesn't sound right," then we need a more sophisticated knowledge of the regularities associated with a language that make it predictable for a reader and thereby easier to interpret.

There are at least three types of patterns that we should be aware of when working with language learners:

- patterns for using and placing words and phrases in a sentence in order to signal the existence of a text that stretches beyond the boundaries of the sentence (cohesion)

- patterns for the occurrence and co-occurrence of words in the context of specific topics and social situations (lexis)
- patterns for the form and placement of words in relation to their role in a sentence (syntax).

Chapter 5 deals with the first two of these types—cohesion and lexis. Syntax is addressed in Chapter 6.

Creating Flow: The Language of Cohesion

Describing the topic of this chapter as "expectations for language" is somewhat misleading because

Tutoring / Teaching Tip

I have one piece of advice for discussing any of these patterns with second language writers. You will note that I am being very careful not to use the word *rules* here. What I recognize as patterns for English are not the same patterns that Shakespeare recognized; they are also not the same patterns accepted by the writers of the newspaper articles from Nigeria and India in Chapter 2. If you frame your comments as "what I expect is . . ." and not "the rule says . . . ," then it will be clearer that adhering to these patterns has nothing to do with right and wrong and everything to do with appealing to a reader.

what most people really expect is to be able to read a text without stopping to notice the language or having to work to understand it; in short, they expect the text to **flow**. In order for a text to flow, it must be organized in a way that meets the expectations of readers. One way that a writer makes the organization of a text clearer for a reader is through **cohesion**—language that makes the connections between sentences explicit.

Consider these two versions of an introduction to a composition class paper written by an Arab student, Mahmoud. His topic was why Henry David Thoreau chose to live on Walden Pond.

(1) First Draft

[1] Thoreau believed that the woods will revive his morals by making him thinking of the main things in life. [2] Thoreau ran away from his society and lived in the woods for two years. [3] While being there, he experienced lot of new stuff that humans missed it by time. [4] By writing his book Walden, Thoreau wanted to share his experiences with the readers making them live more simply and enjoy their lives.

(2) Final Draft

[1] At the age of twenty-eight, in a revolt against the monotonous machinations and fiscal norms of the society, Henry David Thoreau decided to desert city life into the woods of Massachusetts in a quest for sheer simplicity. [2] _Thoreau believed that the woods would revive his morals_ and enrich his values, _making him think_ solely _of what is truly crucial in life_. [3] _Living_ alone _in the wilderness for more than two years, he experienced new concepts and perspectives that his fellow citizens had been missing on_ living the daily-somewhat fast paced-life of a blooming mining society. [4] Thoreau thus developed a new overall understanding of economic priorities within a delicate spiritual frame that Mother Nature had made him realize.[5] _By writing his book Walden, Thoreau wanted to share his experience with the readers encouraging to live simple_ and open their eyes to what really matters.

The underlined elements in the final draft mark content that appeared in the initial draft. Both versions begin with a claim about what Thoreau believed the woods would offer him, followed by a statement of what he experienced there and his goal of sharing those experiences in the book _Walden_. I would guess though that you have more problems reading the first draft than the final. The final draft contains two additional content elements—_going to the_ *woods equaled a revolt against city life* and *his new understanding of economic priorities*, but these elements are not what improved the flow.

In the first draft, we keep losing our way, only to rediscover it somewhere later in the sentence. Each sentence begins with a claim about Thoreau, but the effect of using a different verb each time (*believed, ran away, experienced,* and *wanted*) is to make the sentences seem like parallel lines that never intersect. The first and second sentences do finally intersect when we realize that the woods that would *revive his morals* were also an opportunity to escape society. This is difficult to figure out though because in the second sentence our thoughts are directed away from *society* before we can enter the *woods* and so we have to make the connection retroactively. The one helpful connector is the phrase *while being there* at the beginning of the third sentence because *there* is the woods. With Sentence 4, however, we have to start off in a totally new location, namely Thoreau's goals for writing the book.

For the final draft, Mahmoud adds a new first sentence that frames the paragraph as a narrative. More important to understanding the original beginning (now Sentence 2), he identifies what woods are being discussed, which makes the use of the definite article in *the woods* (i.e., the ones that he had beliefs about) easier to interpret. He also achieves a smoothing effect by ending Sentence 2 with *in life* and then picking up this thread with *living* at the beginning of Sentence 3. Sentence 4 uses the word *thus* to mark itself as presenting a conclusion that ties together the previous sentences and makes the transition to the claim about the purpose of the book in Sentence 5 less abrupt. Moreover, even though Sentence 5 represents a shift from the events to their significance, it still relates to the previous text by repeating the word *experience*.

Mahmoud's final draft provides examples of four different devices for making a text flow and feel connected:

1. **Referential ties.** When Mahmoud uses *the* before *woods* in Sentence 2, he lets us know that he is giving us more information about *the woods of Massachusetts* mentioned in

Sentence 1. The **definite article** signals a continuing reference to an earlier mentioned entity. **Pronouns** and **demonstrative** words such as *this* or *that* serve a similar function in that they frequently direct a reader's attention to an earlier term in the text and serve to carry it forward in the reader's mind. All three of these devices—definite articles, pronouns, and demonstrative words—use reference to connect the content of a current sentence to previous content and tell us as readers that we are adding, not starting anew.

2. **Information order.** One definition for a sentence is "a group of words that can stand alone." Sentences do not need anything before or after them to make them comprehensible. If the sentence is in a text, however, we really do not want it to stand alone. We want each sentence to build off of what has come before. One way of creating the sense that we are doing this in English is to control the order in which we bring topics into the reader's consciousness. When Mahmoud begins Sentence 3 with *living*, he is picking up the concept of *in life* that finished Sentence 2. He is beginning his new sentence where the previous sentence left off. The effect is to make Sentence 3 seem like an extension of Sentence 2, not a new unit to be processed independently. Consider how the final draft would read if the phrase *living alone in the wilderness for more than two years* were placed at the end of Sentence 3 instead of at the beginning.

Another common pattern for sequencing information is to begin a series of sentences with a reference to a central topic followed by a comment about the topic. This may have been Mahmoud's strategy in his first draft where each sentence begins with *Thoreau*. For this pattern to create flow, however, the comments have to bear a logical relation to each other. In Mahmoud's first draft, they were too independent for a reader to figure out.

3. **Transitional expressions.** Mahmoud's use of *thus* in Sentence 4 is an explicit signal to his readers that this sentence

will present a conclusion that can be drawn from the previous sentences. Transition words (and the related form, conjunctions) express the logical relation that exists between two sections of text. An Internet search for "transition words" will quickly yield lists of expressions categorized according to logical relations such as "sequential" (e.g., *next, then*), "addition" (e.g., *in addition, moreover*), "opposition" (e.g., *however, on the other hand*), "exemplification" (e.g., *for example, as seen in*), and "comparison" (e.g., *similarly, likewise*).

4. **Repetition.** In four of his five sentences, Mahmoud mentions *Thoreau* and uses the word *life* or *living*. He speaks of *simplicity* in Sentence 1 and *simple* in Sentence 5. *Society* appears in Sentences 1 and 3, and *experience(d)* appears in Sentences 3 and 5. Nouns and verbs that signify Thoreau's mental processes (e.g., *think, understanding*) also appear in four of five sentences. There are other examples of the recycling of terms and concepts, but you get the idea. Mahmoud is drawing on the same words and ideas again and again throughout the passage. Although repetition is frequently assumed to make a passage boring or redundant, the effect here is like glue. When a writer reuses vocabulary, it reduces the amount of new vocabulary that a reader must process at the same time that it establishes certain actors and actions as central to the message.

All of these devices employ a type of recycling—either of words or underlying concepts—to hold a passage together. The trick of course is to strike a balance between old and new, to create a forward flow without just going in circles. Consider for a moment this conclusion to another Thoreau paper written by a different student, Ahmed.

[1] <u>In conclusion</u> Thoreau chose to live in a forest for many reasons including to live deleberately and to live a true life. [2] <u>Also</u> Thoreau chose to live in a hut in particular because it's the most suitable place that illustrates Thoreau's definition of life and it is a very close place to nature itself. [3] <u>Moreover</u> Thoreau wanted to look for reality and he wanted to be a part of nature and to be simple as well as conceiving. [4] <u>So</u>, did Thoreau accomplish what he was willing to accomplish in his experience?

As indicated by the expressions underlined at the beginning of each sentence, Ahmed seems to have been taught too much about the usefulness of transitions. In addition, the first two sentences begin with *Thoreau chose to live* and Sentence 3 with the similarly structured *Thoreau wanted to look*. The transitional expressions mark appropriate logical relations and the repetition serves as a frame for the juxtaposition of *many reasons* in Sentence 1 with *in particular* in Sentence 2; nevertheless, I feel almost as if I am stuck in the mud when I read this passage because there is so much glue that the new information is not readily apparent.

If you are working with second language writers, it is important to realize that devices that signal cohesion can be both underused and overused. If students are underusing them, it may be because they are writing one sentence at a time and are primarily focused on the internal structure of their sentences. They may have a plan for what they want to write, but the plan consists of individual points rather than a strategy for moving a reader from one idea to another. If this is the case, it may be helpful to ask them how one sentence relates to another. Ask them if the sentences need to be in their current sequence, and if so, why? You may also want to read the passage aloud for them, pointing out where you are surprised or confused because an idea does not build off the previous.

If a student is overusing cohesive devices, then he or she may be struggling to find something new to write; or he or she may be mechanistically applying a lesson learned in an English class, as seems to be the case with Ahmed's transitional expressions. Either way, the first step is to get rid of the unnecessary phrasing so that you can focus on whether more content needs to be invented. Point out that some connections can be inferred and also that variety is the spice of life—that is, do not just use transitions. Also, if students are using the same frame multiple times as with Ahmed's *Thoreau chose to live*, suggest combining the two sentences into one.

Lexis: The Right Word at the Right Time

The second expectation that readers have for language relates to the writer's choice of words. When I mention **word choice**, you might think I mean knowing what a word means, its dictionary definition. Clearly knowing words that represent specific meanings is a significant issue for language learners, and assessing vocabulary size is one of the best means for distinguishing a language learner from a native speaker. With the exception of an occasional instance where a student mixes the meanings of two similar words or receives a bad suggestion from an online translator, knowing the dictionary entry for a word is not something you will need to address while working on writing, however. If

I disagree

Tutoring / Teaching Tip

Transitional expressions are extremely problematic for language learners because the logical relations that they encapsulate are usually much more complex than the charts in grammar books would suggest. Searching the Internet for a list of transitional expressions is useful because it shows students the range of possibilities, but it is not sufficient. For example, *moreover* and *furthermore* both signal continuance, but they are not interchangeable. The Internet also offers examples of the expressions being used in texts. Ask students to explain the relation signaled in texts you find. It is useful to compare the way different transitions with a related meaning are used and also to find multiple examples. When looking at the examples, notice how the transitions are punctuated. Some transitional expressions occur primarily at the beginning of new sentences, others in the middle of a sentence set off by commas, others after commas or semi-colons. You built up your knowledge of the patterns associated with these words through multiple exposures; learners need the same.

students do not know what a word means, they are unlikely to use it when writing. For writing, the big issues tend to be malformed words and words that just do not seem appropriate. Word formation will be addressed in Chapter 6 on syntax because more often than not this relates to the role the word plays in the sentence. For the purposes of this chapter, I want to focus on why a word might sound strange or funny or simply wrong in a given context.

Consider these two paragraphs written as the introduction and conclusion to the first draft of a paper reacting to an article about environmental dangers in the Middle East. I have removed some of the words that the student, Marwan, used. Are you able to predict what you think would fill the blanks?

"Desertification, urban growth, transport, fresh water supply, energy consumption, agricultural productivity and pollution" all of these are issues which the whole (1) _*enviro* is facing. Since time immemorial, humans were one of the main causes of many environmental problems. Their affect can be directly and indirectly, and at the end, it may end up (2a) _____ the environments as much as its (2b) _____ it. Many huge issues are made just because of the (3) _____ of the human beings. Governments were aware about that previously, but what they did was almost like ignoring what (4) _____. Many studies proves that "the share of expenditure by local authorities on preserving the environment, compared with total state expenditure, is among the lowest in world.

In conclusion, these issues are currently (5) _____ day after day, which is causing the harm for the current generation and the generations to come. Various types of environmental pollutions occur every day, and (6) _____ studies are trying to protect the current healthy environments. Are those studies are really going to help? And if they do, will the people then stop polluting it again?

My predictions are: (1) *world*, (2a) *hurting*, (2b) *helps*, (3) *needs*, (4) *was happening*, (5) *getting worse*, and (6) *many*. You may have made different predictions, but my choices should not sound strange.

Now read the original version of these two paragraphs.

> "Desertification, urban growth, transport, fresh water supply, energy consumption, agricultural productivity and pollution" all of these are issues which the whole (1) <u>universe</u> is facing. Since time immemorial, humans were one of the main causes of many environmental problems. Their affect can be directly and indirectly, and at the end, it may end up (2a) <u>affecting</u> the environments as much as its (2b) <u>benefits</u> it. Many huge issues are made just because of the (3) <u>benefit</u> of the human beings. Governments were aware about that previously, but what they did was almost like ignoring (4) <u>what was going on</u>. Many studies proves that "the share of expenditure by local authorities on preserving the environment, compared with total state expenditure, is among the lowest in world."
>
> In conclusion, these issues are currently (5) <u>increasing</u> day after day, which is causing the harm for the current generation and the generations to come. Various types of environmental pollutions occur every day, and (6) <u>a bunch of</u> studies are trying to protect the current healthy environments. Are those studies are really going to help? And if they do, will the people then stop polluting it again?

All of the underlined words are comprehensible, well formed, and marked appropriately for tense or agreement, but they are not what I would have written in this context.

There are at least two explanations for why not, and the first has to do with the sheer frequency to which I have been exposed to Marwan's word choices. In Sentence 1, the word *whole* commonly occurs with both Marwan's *universe* and my *world*. If you do an Internet search for the two phrases, however, the expression *whole world* is much more common than *whole universe*. This may be because the former is used to refer to the physical earth as well as to generalize about the people on it, while the latter is used primarily to refer to the physical cosmos. In Sentence 2, the conjunction *as much as* is likewise commonly used to join the opposites *hurt* and *help*. Marwan must be aware of this pattern, but he does not realize that substitutions are not allowed. His synonyms for *hurt* and *help* (*affect* and *benefit*) just do not sound like anything I have ever heard.

Sentence 3 is a little more problematic. Marwan could have said *many issues are made just to benefit human beings*, but his choice of the prepositional phrase *because of* requires the noun *benefit*, not the infinitive *to benefit*. He uses the appropriate noun form, but he does not realize that we interpret his new construction *the benefit of human beings* to mean why it is good to have human beings (cf., *human beings' benefit*), not what is good for human beings (cf., *human beings need*). The phrase, *the benefit of* _____, is common, but Marwan has not figured out its nuances.

The issue in Sentence 5 is somewhat similar. If I do an Internet search for *are increasing day after day* I find a lot of examples that start with *the numbers of* ____. If I do an Internet search for *these issues are increasing,* I find that it is often followed by either a statement of what is increasing (e.g., *doubts*) or a phrase with *in* such as *in significance* that tells how they are increasing. Marwan's construction draws from both of these patterns but fits into neither. Finally, when I use an Internet search to compare Marwan's *issues are increasing* with my suggestion of *issues are getting worse,* I find five times as many examples of my choice as his.

One important comment: When I say that these choices are determined by frequency, I mean the frequency with which words co-occur with other words. Probably if you studied vocabulary in school, you had to learn the word's part of speech and definition and then be able to use it in a sentence. In reality, this is a very small part of the information that the brain attaches to words. What native speakers of a language get through repeated exposure to words in use is a sense of the environments where the word seems to be useful and where many people tend to use it. That environment may be indicated by other words (e.g., *whole* with *world*) or topics (e.g., *issues* are more likely to *get better or worse* than *to increase*). The technical term for this sense that a word is more likely to occur in some environments than others is **collocation.**

For Sentences 4 and 6 there is a different explanation for the sense that they are not appropriate for this essay. Marwan's paper was written for an academic class, and it is important, therefore, that he sound "academic." But these word choices make him sound like he is having a conversation with friends. The problem with Sentence 4 starts with the modifier *almost like* and continues with the phrasal verb *going on*. In Sentence 6, the use of *a bunch of* will be read by many readers just as it is usually pronounced, "abuncha." These expressions are more likely to occur in informal speech than written, informational or expository texts. As noted in Chapter 2, Generation 1.5 students frequently have more practice with the language of informal social interactions than written texts and are often described as "writing like they talk." Marwan has primarily studied in foreign language settings. Nevertheless, he too has somehow learned good conversational skills whether through travel, television, or international friends at school, and he is relying on them when he writes. Now, however, he has to learn to distinguish between the language of McDonald's® and the language of the library. *HORRIBLE*

FALSE

Sentences 4 and 6 are examples of register problems. Whereas collocation problems are signaled by the words around a given word, register issues relate to the social purpose that a text serves. Many words and phrases can be used as easily in conversation as in a business letter, but others immediately conjure up images of specific social situations. How easily can you imagine a text where would you expect to find *esteemed, aforementioned,* or *dude*? When I read these words, I think of a formal declaration, a legal document, and a teen magazine, respectively. This kind of association between language and social situations can be particularly problematic for language learners who have less familiarity with the ways social situations are divided up in the target culture. They probably understand the difference between formal and informal language in principle, but they do not know which situations are formal and which are informal. They may also have problems with which words are associated with particular registers and which are common across a range of registers.

Teaching Lexis

Marwan's essay provides us examples of problematic word choices that are even more problematic to explain. Our expectations for words that are different from Marwan's are based in our experience with the language, not in a rule that we can find in a writer's handbook. My explanations for you may be more involved than you want to try to get into with a student, especially when that is not the only issue you need to address in the paper. How you handle instances like these depends on how much time you have to focus on one issue and also how serious you think the problem is.

The quickest response is to simply supply a more appropriate word or phrase. You have probably been told that you should not "correct" student papers, that it is important for students to feel ownership of what goes into their papers, and that they will not learn if you do the work for them. All of this is sound advice. If the problem that led to the inappropriate choice of words is insufficient exposure, however, then providing the student with a more target-like expression at least begins to correct that problem. It may not be a change that they will understand why it needs to happen, but at the very least they may remember the word the next time they encounter it. You have made the expression salient for them and identified it as a vocabulary item that they need to investigate further.

If you have more time to focus on word choice issues, then help students with that investigation. For a collocation problem, let them know which words you find problematic and suggest that they investigate whether these expressions are regularly used and, if so, in what contexts. Today's Internet search engines allow you to search for an intact phrase by putting it in quotation marks. They also generally include a count of how many instances of the search term were found. If the expression never shows up, learners should immediately realize that an alternative is needed. If it shows up, however, learners need to pay attention to the topical context as well as the type of documents where it seems most frequent. Because you also want to expose them to a more appropriate wording, you should also ask them to search for what you think would be a better alternative. Ask them to compare the frequency of the alternative phrase with the original. Ask them also to notice the topical content and social purposes for the documents that show up in the different results.

With register difficulties, you will need to figure out whether they misjudged the social context for their papers or they did not realize the social markings of the language per se. If the issue is the social context for the paper, then much of the advice in Chapter 3 related to understanding the assignment and the audience is relevant. Talk to them about why they are writing, who they are writing for, and how they want that audience to react to the paper. If the issue is the social indexing of the language, then again try to direct them toward examples and ask them to infer the characteristics of the contexts where these words occur.

Tutoring / Teaching Tip

One useful resource for helping students recognize language that is primarily oral and/or informal is the Michigan Corpus of Academic Spoken English (http://quod.lib.umich.edu/m/micase). This online resource provides transcripts of more formal and less formal oral conversations in academic settings. Seeing that a phrase is more commonly used during office hours than during a group presentation will help learners understand the way in which the word is used as well as possibly enrich their knowledge of the social continua that cut across academia.

6

Syntax: The Big, the Bad, and the Ugly

Chapter 5 argued that readers expect texts to be cohesive, employ appropriate lexis, and adhere to syntactic patterns. Of these, **syntax** is the area that we most notice when it goes awry. Marking cohesion and choosing appropriate lexical items make texts more palatable for a reader; they help us fit the pieces together and confirm hypotheses about the social purposes of the text. They are the grease that speeds interpretation and are worth addressing with a student because they make a piece of writing better. Syntax, on the other hand, is an issue that we must address because it can lead a reader to give up even trying to understand a text. What is your reaction to this sentence taken from the beginning of a paper evaluating the applications of nanotechnology?

> Advantages in nanotechnology have the potential to completely update many aspects of medicine and health care, includes developing very rapid gene sequencing devices, and it will make each individual therapy possible.

We can work to figure out what the student probably wanted to say, but in the real world you would probably have to be a professor needing to assign a grade or extremely interested in this topic to keep reading. Unfortunately, however, many of us shy away from addressing syntactic issues with students because we feel that they are too complex to explain or learn.

This chapter discusses what we mean by syntactic patterns and how they contribute to interpretation of meaning. It then suggests a three-step process for addressing syntactic issues with second language writers. Along the way you will find a basic review of grammar terminology and a number of examples of problematic constructions from student papers.

The Nature of the Beast

In Chapter 5, I defined syntax as "patterns for the form and placement of words in relation to their role in a sentence." If you loathe discussing syntax with a student, it may be because of long hours you spent in English classes learning to label "roles" in meaningless sentences. You learned to apply terms like *subject, predicate, noun, adjective, interjection, dependent clause, appositive,* and *adverbial adjunct,* but you did not learn anything that helped you do more with a language you already knew how to put together with a certain degree of automaticity. This exercise is actually very similar to the process we follow every time we read a sentence, however—a process whereby we identify units of language and attach meanings to them. And if we are working with language learners, it is very helpful to recognize and be able to explain our processes for constructing and deconstructing sentences.

Here is a sentence taken from the last essay shown in Chapter 5 by Marwan:

> In conclusion, these issues are currently increasing day after day, which is causing the harm for the current generation and the generations to come.

It starts with a group of words set off from the rest of the sentence by a comma—*in conclusion.* You may have learned to label this group as a "prepositional phrase used as a conjunct." But what does that mean? First of all, **prepositional phrases** are multifunctional units in English that generally serve to modify or limit another expression. We recognize them by the occurrence of an item from a relatively small set of words (e.g., *in, on, at, from, before*) followed by a second word belonging to a much larger set known as **nouns.** The fact that this prepositional phrase can be separated easily from the rest of the sentence and also moved around to multiple positions within the sentence (cf., *these issues, in conclusion, are currently . . .*) indicates to us that its meaning is peripheral to the rest of the sentence. In this case, it is used to link the meaning of the rest of the sentence to what has come before, hence the label **conjunct.**

Consider the next group of words—*these issues.* A linkage exists in our minds between *these* and three other words: *this, that, those.* These terms, traditionally labeled as **demonstratives,** are used as a guide to whether we should interpret another term or concept as proximal or distant. They may serve as a stand-in for a concept (i.e., a pronoun) that has been referred to already (e.g., *these are delicious*) or as the indicator of the frame of reference for a term that follows, as in *these issues.* If we look up *issue* in a dictionary, we find that it can have a verbal meaning "to send out" or a nominal meaning "topic or problem." The fact that it follows *these* points us immediately toward the second interpretation. Figuring this out is actually a fairly complex process, however. Since demonstratives can serve as stand-ins for a concept, they can function as subjects of verbs. The *-s* on the end of *issue* could mean that it is a verb, but only if the subject of the verb is singular. The fact that we have *these* and not *this* or *that*, therefore, helps us rule out the possibility of *issues* being a verb. Further confirmation of our hypothesis comes when the next word we encounter—*are*—is a verb in need of a concept that can function as its instigator (i.e., subject).

This may be more than you ever wanted to read about the English language and its workings. The point though is that the patterns associated with syntax make extended communication possible. Using specialized words such as prepositions and demonstratives, permutations on the form of a word (e.g., *issue/issues*), and conventions for what it means when one kind of word occurs before or after another (e.g., a noun after a preposition creates a unit that can modify or limit other expressions), English encodes concepts such as how many, who instigated what, which one, and what action should we focus on. This kind of meaning, often referred to as grammatical or syntactic meaning, is essential to turning dictionary meanings into a message.

One caveat before we begin discussing the needs of second language writers: It is important to recognize that these patterns for encoding syntactic meaning are both arbitrary and mutable. English distinguishes between one instance of a countable concept (*issue*) and more than one (*issues*); other languages such as classical Arabic make a three-way distinction between one instance, two instances, and more than two. Whereas English marks verbal actions as starting in the past, present, or future, other languages mark them simply as completed or unfinished. There is a lot of overlap in the syntactic meaning that languages encode, but we cannot assume that an English language learner will have the same set of underlying concepts that we have.

Similarly, compare this sentence with the first example in this chapter about the advantages of nanotechnology:

> I discovered many a site for a house not likely to be soon improved, which some might have thought too far from the village, but to my eyes the village was too far from it.

With both examples, the concatenation of expressions makes it very easy to lose sight of what *it* is. The first example was written by a first-semester student in a first-year composition class for non-native speakers; the second was written by Henry David Thoreau in the second chapter of *Walden*. What seems "right" today may seem antiquated or strained tomorrow. Nothing makes a pattern innately or eternally correct.

Finally, consider this sentence from Rena's essay discussed in Chapter 4:

> It is important to have belonging to one nationality as it is important to have loyalty toward one country.

The sentence sounds strange to me, and I can suggest a number of possible ways to change it, but I also cannot say that I do not understand it. I wish the sentence had signaled that it was a comparison by beginning with *as*. I also would find *to belong* easier to interpret than *to have belonging*, but then the parallelism with *have loyalty* would be lost. There are patterns that, when violated, render the sentence impossible for me to interpret; there are other usages, such as Rena's, which I can only label as infelicitous.

I like to think of syntactic patterns as being mutually agreed upon conventions for assembling dictionary meanings. The certainty I feel toward the convention derives directly from my experience, and I may even change my opinion over time (the Holy Grail for many grade school English teachers). Thus, as with many other writing issues, we have to frame discussions of syntax in terms of what we are used to, not what is right. We also have to be able to accept multiple possibilities for encoding and gradient convictions about the need for change.

Slaying the Dragon

Syntax has the potential to overwhelm and sidetrack any discussion with students about their writing. Often multiple problems will be noted in every sentence; and just as it took a whole paragraph to explain how we understand what *these issues* means, justifying our concerns over just one phrase can leave a student still confused after ten minutes. Figuring out when and how to address syntax, therefore, is crucially important. The general principle advocated in this book is to address the big picture—meeting the goals of the assignment and organizing a coherent argument—before turning to syntax. Unless you have a particularly opportune teaching moment, you probably do not want to waste your time or the students' changing language that should not be in the paper to begin with.

Once you have made the decision to address syntax, however, I suggest a three-step process:

1. Isolate the issues.
2. Select which ones to address.
3. Choose a method for addressing them.

I will discuss each of these steps and along the way will provide a quick refresher course as to how some of those labels learned in the distant past actually impact interpretation. We will also consider how the syntax of a language is learned.

Isolate the Issues

Linguists employ a variety of models to explain syntactic patterning in languages. My thinking has been most influenced by a model that recognizes three hierarchically nested levels of structure: the word, the phrase, and the clause. With English, we can identify at each of these levels a central item that allows and/or requires certain other items before and after it. Look at Marwan's sentence again:

> In conclusion, these issues are currently increasing day after day, which is causing the harm for the current generation and the generations to come.

A number of the words in this sentence can be seen as constructed: examples are *conclusion* = *con* + *clus* + *ion*; *issues* = *issue* + *s*; *currently* = *current* + *ly*; *increasing* = *in* + *crease* + *ing*. In each case there is a root item that allows prefixes and/or suffixes to be added to it. Similarly, we recognize phrases like *in conclusion, are currently increasing,* and *to come* and two clauses *these issues are currently increasing day after day* and *which is causing the harm for the current generation and the generations to come.* It may be more difficult with phrases and clauses to identify the central item, but we can still recognize the power that one item exerts over others. While I can write *in conclusion,* I cannot write *in conclude.* I also cannot write *which causing the harm* or *which the harm is causing* and have it mean the same thing.

Language learners run into problems when they do not have a firm grasp of these co-occurrence conditions—when they put the wrong suffix on a root (as in *currention*), when after a preposition they put a verb form instead of a noun (as in *in conclude*), when they omit the word that marks the time reference for a clause (as in *these issues currently increasing day after day*), or when they put the object before the verb (as in *which the harm is causing*). It would be nice if student essays were like a web page where, if a feature does not display correctly, we can diagnose the problem by switching our browser to the underlying html code used to create the page. With language learners, unfortunately, we cannot just tell our word processers to display the syntactic patterns applied to create a sentence; we must make an educated guess at them. The process I suggest is to start by considering whether an issue affects the word, phrase, or clause level.

The next discussion lists some high-frequency issues for second language writers at each of these levels. The discussion of each issue is followed by examples written by five different students (labeled A–E). The complete paragraphs from which the examples are taken are reproduced on pages 108–11.

Word Level

Broadly speaking, there are two types of words: **lexical words** that refer to concepts, processes, or qualities and **grammatical words** such as pronouns, articles, auxiliary verbs, and conjunctions that primarily signal a syntactic relation. Each type presents its own specialized problems.

- **Derivations.** Lexical words frequently are constructed from roots surrounded by prefixes and suffixes. In English the prefixes generally modify the referential meaning of the root, whereas suffixes simply mark the word as a noun (*-ion, -ity, -ness*), verb (*-ize, -en, -fy*), adjective (*-ic, -al, -able*), or adverb (*-ly*). Sometimes you get words where multiple prefixes and suffixes are added on (*de + nat + ion + al + ize*), giving the appearance that the word has been "derived" from another. The process for getting from A to D is not random, however.

You cannot say *denation or denational,* only *denationalize.* Similarly, you cannot skip a step; neither *denatalize* or *denationize* make sense. These complexities make derivationally created lexical words potentially difficult for learners who may misconstrue the effect a prefix will have on a root, associate the wrong part of speech with a suffix, or skip a step when deriving the word.

Examples: (<u>Note</u>: The letters after each example indicate which student paper on pages 108–11 the selection is from.)

1. *that an average of 27,600 dollars <u>indebtness</u> is too much for a student* (A)
2. *This form a heavy <u>responsible</u>* (A)
3. *concern that the nanotechnology brings is not yet the environmental <u>impaction</u>* (E)

- **Multi-word words.** Learners may also have problems knowing what constitutes a word in English. Just as *denationalize* may be seen as a string of smaller units of meaning that combine to form one meaning, there are strings of separate words that seem to function more as a single unit than as independent players. Think about *walk in, record player, because of,* and *even if.* Each of these expressions can be decomposed into individual meanings just like *denationalize* can, but our sense that they are separate words is primarily based on the way they are represented on paper. You can substitute the word *enter* for almost every usage of *walk in.* You can have a *big record player* or a *green record player* but not a *record big player.* Compare *because of these reasons* with *in conclusion*; *because of* seems to function exactly like the preposition *in.* Similarly *even if* has a more nuanced meaning than *if* by itself, but they will occur in exactly the same environments; it is hard to separate the semantic contribution of *even* from that of *if.*

  Frequently linguists look at these multi-word "words" as evidence of how the language has evolved over time. What may originally have been independent words now have been used together so frequently that speakers of the language consider them as a single unit. Some such expressions even begin to be written as single words (e.g., *moreover*). Other expressions, like *record player*, actually encode a complex relation between the two items (cf., *a device that plays records*). For language learners, these constructions are problematic because they are written as independent words instead of a single unit, often have related single word forms that function differently (e.g., *because of* and *because*), and may encode a complex relation equivalent to a clause but where the words would be in a different order. Learners may omit or make inappropriate substitutions for parts of the string, wrongly associate the string with the function of one of the component parts, reverse the order, or create strings that are not accepted as strings for common usage.

Examples:

1. *People have to give up their time, work and pay <u>school's fee</u>* (A)
2. *to be in debt by taking <u>the education's loan</u> which supports their <u>college's life</u>* (A)
3. *This form a heavy responsible in <u>debt term</u>* (A)
4. *In fact, <u>even</u> the loan getting higher, more students put themselves indebtness to have a high education* (A)

• **Inflections.** Finally, English uses a small set of word endings and permutations on the form of a word to indicate syntactic meanings. These markings are known as inflections and they signal number on nouns (*-s, this/these, that/those*), the person and number of the subject of a verb (*-s, am/is/are, was/were, have/has*), the temporal frame of reference and state for a verb (*-ed, -en, is/was, break/broke*), and comparison with an adjective (*-er, -est*). Inflections that reflect number or person are said to **agree** with the word that signals the number and/or person.

Languages differ considerably in the extent and type of syntactic meaning that they mark with inflections. Concepts like person, number, and even time are not always that important to understanding the primary message of a text or they may be marked in multiple ways already. If the subject *it* is written out, why does the verb also need to indicate that the subject is third person singular? Or what about *two teachers*—why do we need *-s* if we have *two*? Whether the cause is a first language pattern or a failure to see the need, learners frequently omit or misapply inflections.

Examples:

1. *This <u>form</u> a heavy responsible* (A)
2. *1.5 billion people in the world <u>suffers</u> from extreme poverty* (B)
3. *These statistics really <u>requires</u> people to act* (B)
4. *The similarities between <u>this</u> two ads* (C)
5. *<u>This</u> young attractive models* (C)
6. *I am responsible and neat student that <u>make</u> me a hard and good student* (D)
7. *The <u>most</u> concern* (E)
8. *take every advantage of the nanotechnology that <u>benefit</u> our society* (E)

Phrase Level

In the hierarchy of a clause, phrases are a level of structure above the word. They consist of one or more words that function as a single unit within the larger clause (or text). They are classified according to the part of speech of a central word around which they are constructed and that determines their function. Frequently, one phrase may be nested inside of another phrase. This diagram parses the opening conjunct plus the two clauses of Marwan's sentence. The part of speech after the final bracket indicates a phrase's function.

(1)

[In conclusion]$_{preposition}$,

(2)

[these issues]$_{noun}$ $\Big[$are [currently]$_{adverb}$ increasing [day after day]$_{adverb}$ $\Big]_{verb}$

(3)

[which]$_{pronoun\ used\ as\ noun}$ $\Big[$is causing [the harm [for [the [current]$_{adjective}$ generation]$_{noun}$ and [the generations[to come]$_{infinitive}$]$_{noun}$]$_{preposition}$]$_{noun}$ $\Big]_{verb}$

The sentence begins with *in conclusion,* a prepositional phrase that connects the meaning of the two clauses that comprise the rest of the sentence to the meaning of the text. In the first clause, *these issues* is a noun phrase that functions as the subject of the verb, and *are currently increasing day after day* is a verb phrase with two adverb phrases nested inside of it. The phrasal layers in the second clause are even more complex. The verb phrase that begins with *is* has a noun phrase (*the harm . . . to come*) as its object. The noun phrase contains a prepositional phrase (*for . . . to come*). The preposition *for* is completed by two separate noun phrases, one of which has an adjective phrase (*current*) embedded in it and the other of which has an infinitive (*to come*) completing the meaning of the noun (*generations*). It may seem strange to call single words such as *current* a phrase, but it is a way of recognizing that this is a slot in a larger unit that could be expanded if the writer so desired. For example, the adjective phrase *current* could be expanded to *most current.*

For language learners, the issue is that each of these central nouns, prepositions, verbs, adverbs, and adjectives places constraints on the type of words that can or must come before and after it in the phrase. Sometimes the constraint is common to all instances of that part of speech (e.g., prepositions must be followed by a noun phrase), and sometimes the constraint is idiosyncratic to the particular lexical item (e.g., *cause* must be followed by a noun phrase; it cannot be followed by nothing; it cannot be followed by just a prepositional phrase). Further complicating the process, when there is extensive *nesting* as in the second clause, the words that satisfy the constraint may be far removed from the word that placed the constraint. It is impossible to list all the constraints that lexical items place on each other at the phrasal level, so I want to concentrate on some general constraints affecting verb phrases and noun phrases.

- **The aftermath of verbs.** All verbs marked for temporality in English must be preceded by subjects. There is wide variety, however, in what follows them. They can be followed by nothing (*these issues are increasing*), one noun phrase (*it is causing the harm*), two noun phrases (*it is causing them the harm*), a noun phrase plus a prepositional phrase (*it is causing the harm for generations*), a prepositional phrase alone (*he is looking out the window*), an adjective (*the pie smells good*), a clause (*she believes that the earth is round*), a noun phrase plus a clause (*she believes him that the earth is round*), and the list could go on. Key here is that while many verbs allow for multiple finishes, they usually will not accept all.

  Thus, language learners may encounter the word *feel* and quickly infer from the context that it means something similar to *believe*. They realize that just as they can say *she believes that the earth is round*, they can also say *she feels that the earth is round*. What they probably will not realize, however, is that although they can say *she believes him that the earth is round*, they cannot say *she feels him that the earth is round*. Another frequent problem is deciding if a meaning such as directionality is part of the verb or needs to be encoded separately in a preposition that follows; thus *walk into the class* might prompt a learner by analogy to write *attend into the class*.

  Examples:

  1. *it does not <u>stop them taking an education's loan</u>* (A)
  2. *to <u>attend into</u> a college* (A)

3. *I would like to <u>attend to</u> this college. I have <u>done well my education</u> in HCCS* (D)
4. *I introduce myself to you to <u>enroll for this college</u>.* (D)
5. *I know that to get a good image from your college will make me <u>get confident</u>* (D)
6. *small group of people can <u>cause of thousands</u> of people to the end of their life* (E)
7. *what we do and <u>how we do today</u>* (E)

- **Determination of nouns.** The possible structure for noun phrases can be depicted as a series of four slots:

Determiner	Adjective Phrase(s)	Noun	Post-Modifiers
the a each one my this	current older very big extremely pretty	generation	at this time that we have discussed following this one to follow
the many two our these		generations	

Adjective phrases and post-modifiers elaborate on the qualities of the noun and so are only filled if we want to elaborate. The difference between the two is that adjective phrases are built around single-word adjectives, whereas post-modifiers are prepositional phrases or clauses. For language learners, the first slot is the one that tends to be most problematic. It belongs to a class of words known as determiners. This slot must be filled if the noun is a countable noun like *generation*. If the noun is an uncountable noun like *humanity*, then filling it is optional.

As a class, determiners mark one of four syntactic meanings: definiteness, quantity, possession, or proximity. By far the most common choice in English is to mark definiteness. In prototypical cases, definiteness equates to whether the reader can be assumed by the writer to have a specific, soon-to-be specific, or generic referent in mind for the noun. Unfortunately, the system for marking these distinctions is very problematic for learners because there is no one-to-one correspondence between marker and meaning. Instead, there are four options, all but one of which can signal multiple categories of referents:

1. **definite article**
   a. specific: *the generation we discussed*
   b. generic: *the generation is a useful unit for measuring time*

2. **indefinite article**
   a. soon-to-be specific: *a generation you might find interesting*
   b. generic: *a generation is a useful unit for measuring time*

3. **plural inflection**
   a. generic: *generations are a useful unit for measuring time*
   b. soon-to-be specific: *generations you might find interesting*

4. **definite article + plural inflection**
   a. specific: *the generations we discussed*

Further compounding this complexity, uncountable nouns can be marked with the definite article (*she saw the humanity in his face*) but not the indefinite.

When trying to isolate the issue in a learner's paper, decide first if the noun needs to be singular or plural or it does not matter. Then, make sure there is a determiner if the noun is countable (remembering that a plural marker can satisfy this condition). Finally, if the choice is to mark definiteness, consider what you can be expected to know about the referent for the noun from the context.

Examples:

1. *I can contribute to this college in the future. When I get the good job, you can be proud of me* (D)
2. *I am responsible and neat student* (D)
3. *I have schedule of my major* (D)
4. *Efficient drug discovery and new way of delivering medicine into human body* (E)
5. *nanotechnology will also has the significant impacts on energy efficiency* (E)
6. *it can be used to supervise and fix environmental problem* (E)
7. *small group of people can cause of thousands of people to the end of their life* (E)
8. *with the nanotechnology new weapon could definitely be much (adverb formation) powerful than what we have currently* (E)
9. *it is not too late to prevent negative impact on the nanotechnology* (E)
10. *but it is not too late to exercise the control* (E)

Clause Level

Although we typically talk about sentences as the highest level of syntactic patterning, the clause is actually a much easier unit to identify. Clauses are constructed around a verb phrase (or occasionally a series of conjoined verb phrases with a single subject). If the verb is marked for temporality, we call the clause **finite**. Finite clauses must have an explicit subject in English and may or may not function as a sentence. If they can stand alone as a sentence, they are considered **independent clauses**; if they cannot stand alone, they are considered **dependent**. Dependent clauses function like nouns, adjectives, or adverbs in the sentence where they are embedded.

independent:

These issues are currently increasing.

dependent:

> *The issues <u>that the report identified</u> are increasing.*
> *(adjective)*
>
> *<u>What is increasing most</u> is the issue of global warming.*
> *(noun)*
>
> *<u>Wherever you look</u>, these issues are increasing.*
> *(adverb)*

If the verb is not marked for temporality, the clause is considered to be **non-finite**. In written English, non-finite clauses typically do not function as independent sentences; rather they serve nominal, adjectival, and adverbial functions within the context of a finite clause. The easiest way to categorize these clauses is according to the form taken by the non-finite verb: V-*ing*, V-*en*, or *(to)* V.

1. **V-*ing***. Non-finite clauses built around the -*ing* form of the verb can function as nouns, adjectives, or adverbs in English. As nouns, a usage traditionally labeled as a **gerund**, they can be the subject or object of a verb or the object of a preposition. Interestingly, with nominal uses, the verb sometimes will have an optional noun phrase before it that resembles a subject as shown in the following example. *noun*

   > Nominal (gerund): <u>*(The bank's) increasing your revenue*</u> *will be difficult.*

   The adjectival usage of *V-ing* is similar to an adjectival dependent clause without the subject or temporality marker. Note that the noun being described by the adjectival clause also resembles a subject for the non-finite verb.

   > Adjectival: *The issues <u>emerging from the discussions</u> surprised us all.*

   Adverbial *V-ing* clauses tend to be set apart in the sentence and may or may not begin with a temporal expression such as *when* or *upon*.

Adverbial: *(When) walking toward town, she found a field full of flowers.*

2. **V-*en*.** Non-finite clauses constructed around the -*en* form of the verb have a more restricted usage. They usually occur after a noun, which is the recipient of the action expressed by the non-finite verb. As with the -*ing* adverbial clauses, however, they may also be pulled out as a type of clausal modifier.

> *The letter written by Disraeli brought a huge sum at auction.*

> *(If) prepared correctly, the cake is absolutely delicious.*

3. **(*to*) V.** The final form of non-finite clauses uses the base form of the verb preceded sometimes by *to*, a form traditionally called an **infinitive**. Infinitives primarily function like the object of a verb but occasionally serve as subjects too. Whether *to* is needed seems to be controlled by the verb of the main clause (e.g., *make* does not allow *to*).

Object: *She wanted (for me) to know the truth.*

Object: *Their words made me realize my mistake.*

Subject: *(For us) to run out of paper would be disastrous.*

As a syntactic unit, clauses link verbal actions and states to actors and recipients of those actions and states, and we generally see them as expressing a more complete thought than words or phrases. In written language, we modulate the significance of these relations to our overall message by switching back and forth between the various levels of clause structure (i.e., independent, dependent, and non-finite). As you might imagine, the problems for language learners arise from embedding these relations in one another and stringing them together.

- **Joining clauses.** If you have ever written a paper for an English teacher, then odds are you are familiar with the terms *run-on sentence* and *fragment*. These labels indicate problems with the way we have joined clauses to each other, and they are common in both first and second language writing. In first language writing, the problem is frequently the way the clauses are represented on paper. If we read the text aloud it sounds fine, but on paper there is a missing period or a period where we need a comma (more about this in the next chapter).

Sometimes, though, the problem is the language used to signal the end of one clause or the beginning of the next. Occasionally, first language writers get so caught up in the flow of the language that they try to use what has to be the object of one sentence as the subject of the next. This is a more common issue for language learners who may be struggling to find words at the same time they are trying to figure out if the demands of each verb for subjects and objects have been met. Language learners may also fail to use words like *which* or *that*, words that do little more than signal that a dependent clause is beginning. Finally in a problem akin to the cohesion issues discussed in Chapter 5, they may fail to signal an obligatorily marked logical transition between two clauses.

Examples:

1. *He argues the education's loan is higher than it was <u>before that</u> an average of 27,600 dollars indebtness is too much for a student.* (A)
2. *Perhaps, there is no <u>choice for</u> them to be in debt by taking the education's loan* (A)
3. *when one of every six people is not meeting his daily needs and <u>that</u> is threatened by <u>death makes</u> the problem seriously dangerous* (B)
4. *The first one and most obvious one is that they are both similar <u>products; that</u> deal with the same form of tanning <u>solution. Which</u> does not require you to be out in the sun for a certain amound of time.* (C)
5. *I am responsible and neat <u>student that</u> make me a hard and good student* (D)

6. *Advantages in nanotechnology have the potential to completely update many aspects of medicine and health care,
includes developing very rapid gene sequencing devices,
and it will make each individual therapy <u>possible. Efficient drug discovery and new way of delivering medicine
into human body, other</u> than having benefit on medicine
and health care, nanotechnology will also has the significant impacts on energy <u>efficiency, it</u> can be used to supervise and fix environmental <u>problem. Such</u> as saving the
energy that wasting on all the industry, and reducing the
pollution.* (E)

- **Finiteness**. As noted, non-finite clauses serve adjectival, nominal, and adverbial functions inside a finite clause. This con-
fluence of verbs can lead to confusion about which ones
need to be marked for temporality and which ones do not.
This is especially problematic for non-finite clauses that
serve as adjectival modifiers. These clauses typically follow
the noun they modify, and so it may look like the verb has a
subject, which may in turn prompt a learner to stick in an *-s*
or a helping verb. Equally difficult is figuring out that
although the noun being modified by the adjectival clause is
not a subject, it still has a semantic relation to the verb. With
the V-*ing* form, the noun acts like an agent for the verb; with
the V-*en* form; it is what is acted upon by the verb.

Examples:

1. *according to Sachs (2005)—an economist <u>work</u> with
international agencies to eliminate poverty* (B)
2. *For example, I have schedule of my major <u>write</u> in my
esqueme paper since my first semester* (D)
3. *Advantages in nanotechnology have the potential to completely update many aspects of medicine and health care,
<u>includes</u> developing very rapid gene sequencing devices*
(E)
4. *Such as saving the energy that <u>wasting</u> on all the industry,
and reducing the pollution.* (E)

- **Temporality**. Finite clauses are distinguished by their use
of temporality markers. English uses helping verbs
(*am/is/are/was/were, has/have/had*), modals (*will, would,
may, might, must, can, could, should, have to, ought to*) and
inflections (*-s, -ed*) to mark temporality or **tense**. In addition
to marking past/present/future, these markers combine with
two additional inflections (*-ing, -en*) to signal the writer's
perspective on whether or not an action is ongoing and
whether or not it should be understood to have happened
prior to another point in time, meanings traditionally
referred to as **aspect**. Tense and aspect are often discussed as
if they were one and the same since saying that a verb is
complete or prior seems pretty close to saying that it happened in the past. They really are not, however, because an
action can be viewed as completed or ongoing in the past,
present, or future, and we can think of times in the past,
present, and future that are prior to other times. These
semantic complexities are further compounded by the introduction of modals that pertain to the likelihood of an event
occurring. Finally, there is the sheer complexity of combining these different markers, which can range from zero to
five as shown in this example:

>   *walk*
>
>   *walked*
>
> They   *are walking*   *to the grocery store on Wednesdays.*
>   *will be walking*
>
>   *have be+en walking*
>
>   *will have be+en walking*

Research has shown that language learners master the complexities of assembling markers fairly early on, but figuring out the meanings associated with different sets of markers is a lifelong process. Part of the difficulty is that many of the sets are used very rarely and so learners do not get much practice with them. Moreover, the distinctions made with respect to temporality, aspect, and modality in English may not correspond to previous systems that students have learned or what makes sense to them.

Examples:

1. *I can contribute to this college in the future. When I get the good job, you can be proud of me; for example, this is the student who <u>studies</u> in this college.* (D)
2. *I <u>will expect</u> to be qualified in your college and work in your team* (D)
3. *nanotechnology <u>will also has</u> the significant impacts on energy efficiency* (E)
4. *if the terrorists <u>is also appear</u> in the time that the nanotechnology weapon <u>already produced</u>, how many people can be killed by just tiny group of people?* (E)
5. *what will happen <u>is depended</u> on what we do and how we do today* (E)

This list of word, phrase, and clausal issues is not exhaustive. If you look at pages 108–11 at the full texts from which the learner examples are taken, you will realize that there are problematic constructions that do not fit any of these categories. Moreover, these five students cannot be said to be representative of all English language learners. Nevertheless, this discussion should provide you with an approach to identifying what bothers you, which is to figure out first the scope of the issue. Compare the learner's construction with what you think would be a more appropriate construction. What changed? Before you zero in on the answer, remember that you may need to try several alternatives. Also, remember that identifying the issues is only the first step to addressing language concerns in a student paper.

Select the Issues to Address

The frequency of problematic constructions varies greatly in the five sample papers on pages 108–11. Some students have two or three per paragraph; some have two or three per line. Deciding which issues to address and which to ignore is never easy. It is very difficult to work with students on papers and then let them walk away, knowing that someone else might still look at their papers and ask why there were so many mistakes in it. It is also frustrating, however, to spend 15 minutes of a 30-minute conference explaining why they need an *-ing* on a verb in the second line and cannot use *the* before the noun on the third line. I have already said that before you even address syntax, you must make sure that the message is in place. In selecting which syntactic issues to address, you need to do the same type of prioritizing.

The first step is to read the entire paper. It is very easy to think that you will correct or flag as you go; often, however, after reading further, you will realize that you misunderstood the student's intent. It is also impossible to prioritize until you have a sense of the whole. Next, look for problematic constructions that significantly impair your understanding of the text. They may occur at a crucial point in the writer's argument or lead you initially to misconstrue what the writer wants to say. In Student A's example paper (page 108), the final sentence seems to present a key summation, yet I have to stop so many times to figure out what he means that I am frustrated, which is not how I want to finish my reading:

> In fact, even the loan getting higher, more students put themselves indebtness to have a high education.

A second thing to look for is issues that are repeated multiple times in a paper. If you go through the student examples provided, you will quickly realize that some students have bigger problems with one issue than others. Student A (page 108) has problems with derivations and multi-word words. Students D and

E (pages 110 and 111) have repeated problems with determiners and temporality. Student C (page 109) has multiple problems with joining clauses. Being able to show learners more than one instance in their writing of a particular problem can really motivate them to figure out the issue.

Finally, weigh the ease with which learners may be able to figure out the issue against your opportunity to work with them on it. Will you have time to offer an explanation if one is needed? Is it something that requires a fairly easy explanation, such as, "this is a third person subject and so you have to put an -s on this verb," or is it going to be more complicated (e.g., a determiner)? In relation to this, consider what students are expecting from you. Will they be receptive if you explain an issue, or will they treat it like most people treat grammar corrections on a graded paper—they read them and promptly forget them? Answering this final set of questions requires more than just a sense of priorities, however; it requires a plan for how you will address syntactic issues.

Choose a Method for Addressing the Issue

In addressing syntactic issues, our first priority needs to be learning, not correcting. Students usually come to us because they want an A on their papers. We have to remember that in academic settings they are probably not writing the paper because someone actually needs the finished product; they are writing to practice and improve their analytic and communication abilities. Our goal with syntax therefore should be to help them figure out the commonly accepted pattern(s) for expressing a particular message in a way that they can generalize to other instances. Three possible approaches for doing this are listed.

1. Indicate that an issue exists.

Writing is a complex process. We have to juggle identifying a message, considering our audience and any guidelines we have, breaking the message into component parts and organizing them, and then representing all these thoughts and goals in language. Each of these mental tasks competes with the others for brain power, and it is often language that pays the price—for both first and second language writers. First language writers, however, who have more certainty about the patterns of the language, are usually able to catch these slips if they take the time to go back and edit their writing. Second language writers, on the other hand, are likely to make more slips and to be less certain whether it is a slip in the first place. Thus, we can often help language learners simply by indicating that a problem exists, by underlining or otherwise flagging it.

In order for this approach to be successful, the issue should be something that learners already know the pattern for or could figure out on their own. Word-level problems especially with inflections often fall into this category. The punctuation of clause boundaries when the language sounds "right" but is misrepresented on paper may be another good candidate for this approach. By flagging these issues, you are making them salient in students' minds and helping them build a mental checklist for future writing. If it is an issue for which they do not know the pattern, you may also be framing a learning problem for them and motivating them to find out.

2. Explain what went wrong.

A second approach is to be more explicit about why a construction is problematic. This approach can be particularly helpful if the construction creates something that can be interpreted but that does not necessarily make sense in the larger context. Consider this example of a problem with joining clauses from Student B's paper (page 109):

> when one of every six people is not meeting his daily needs and <u>that</u> is threatened by <u>death makes</u> the problem seriously dangerous

We could start by telling Student B that every time we read a verb, we try to figure out what its subject is. Then ask Student B to identify the verbs in this sentence. If we next point out that we are not sure what *that* refers to and that we do not think that *death makes the problem dangerous*, Student B will learn something about how we interpret the meaning of clauses and also pinpoint where changes need to be made. Hopefully, Student B would then try to break the sentence into three separate clauses before recombining them. The differences between *-ing* and *-en* on the end of a verb for interpretation of the relation between the verb and its subject (or the noun being described by it if it is a non-finite adjectival clause) are another good candidate for this approach.

It should be noted that this is the approach embodied in the editing guides used by many English teachers, where they create a list of shorthand symbols such as frag=fragment or wc=word choice. When used exclusively for all the problematic constructions in a paper, however, these guides are not necessarily helpful. They do not teach what language means, and they frequently do not help learners figure out what should be done instead.

3. Expose students to what would be appropriate.

The final approach is to focus on what should be done. This may be done in a variety of ways. We can identify an issue as belonging to a particular category and then provide an overview of the system as a whole. Many writing center websites have grammar handouts that serve as references for issues like determiners and verb tenses. You also can provide students with quick, one-line statements of high-visibility constraints that you realize they need to check for in a paper, such as:

- Count nouns must have a determiner.
- Verbs marked for tense must have subjects.
- We have to *do* + [*something*]

Both of these techniques require some explicit knowledge about language and the vocabulary to discuss it, which points back to the discussion in Chapter 2 about previous educational experiences that students may have had. Some students will be quite comfortable analyzing language and applying labels to different components; others will not know what you mean if you say *noun* and *verb*.

If you are uncertain about students' grasp of terminological distinctions or are leery of your own ability to explain something clearly, another approach is to provide what is often called **positive evidence.** You figured out the patterns of English through repeated exposure over time and occasionally hearing that someone did not understand what you said. Language learners do not have the luxury of time. If, however, you can direct them toward multiple examples of a construction, they may be able to see the pattern. This can be especially effective with figuring out the structures that a particular verb (or noun or adjective) allows following it. Ask the student to conduct an Internet search for the verb in question and make a collection of complete sentences that use the term. Ask the student to group the examples and describe the patterns. Then ask if the construction produced fits into any of the groups. An additional advantage of working with authentic examples is that you may encounter a structure similar to what the learner produced but not quite the same and that will help you both understand where they went wrong.

—∞∞—

Some people think of second language writers primarily as students who make errors or who cannot put two words together to form a complete sentence. Because syntax is so important in terms of first impressions, we do students a great disservice when we ignore it. We cannot assume it is impossible to address or that time will take care of it. But we also do second language students a disservice if we discuss language only as a problem and not a resource. We cannot forget that derivations allow us to compact a lot of meaning in a little space. The differences between independent, dependent, and non-finite clauses move some events to the foreground while putting others into the background. Definite articles make crystal clear what we are talking about. Student writers—be they first or second language speakers—need to see the complexities of language as a way of packing more meaning, nuancing a stance, and enhancing a reader's experience.

Example Texts

Student A, reaction to newspaper editorial; first-semester non-native composition course

> Having a high education to make good money is the dream of everyone but it requires people to go to school People have to give up their time, work and pay school's fee to attend into a college. Perhaps, there is no choice for them to be in debt by taking the education's loan, which supports their college's life. Grey Winter raises a good point about this issue through his article in the New York Time newspaper "Loan debt, burden hit worse now" He argues the education's loan is higher than it was before that an average of 27,600 dollars indebtness is too much for a student. This form a heavy responsible in debt term, which makes students stop going to school, Or they try to work more hours during school time to keep down their debt These reasons might take students concern carefully, but it does not stop them taking an education's loan. In fact, even the loan getting higher, more students put themselves indebtness to have a high education.

Student B, first paragraph from a synthesis of articles about global poverty; first-semester non-native composition course

> Every day more than 20,000 die of dire poverty and 1.5 billion people in the world suffers from extreme poverty according to Sachs (2005)—an economist work with international agencies to eliminate poverty. These statistics really requires people to act because when one of every six people is not meeting his daily needs and that is threatened by death makes the problem seriously dangerous. When we justify such a problem, we cannot ignore that it needs solutions. Poverty is a big problem asking for solutions. The solutions to poverty all revolve around one thing; a strong economy.

Student C, second paragraph from comparison of two advertisements; developmental writing course

> The similarities between this two ads are small, but they are there. The first one and most obvious one is that they are both similar products; that deal with the same form of tanning solution. Which does not require you to be out in the sun for a certain amound of time. Both ads use the approache that they are streak free. Both argue that they leave behind a smooth natural look. Both ads have a nice, thin attractive young lady with a very natural looking tan in the middle of the ad. This young attractive models represent what a customer wants to gain after they purchase and then use the product like for instant the way they situate the model in the ad, both are showing off their legs, which are tan, and of course they both have a tan skin color that appeals to all young and old women.

Student D, essay for imaginary college application; community college advanced writing course

To my concern, I would like to attend to this college. I have done well my education in HCCS because I have a good grade in my whole classes that I have taken. I am a hard student, and I try to do the best I can; therefore, I can contribute to this college in the future. When I get the good job, you can be proud of me; for example, this is the student who studies in this college.

I know that to get a good image from your college will make me get confident. In addition, this college is serious in its jobs and concerned about the people who will get in. Therefore, I introduce myself to you to enroll for this college. I will be proud of being in your team; also, its facilities fit what I want to be and do. I am responsible and neat student that make me a hard and good student. For example, I have schedule of my major write in my esqueme paper since my first semester through the final semester to finish the college. Therefore, I am ready to study in your college, and I will be happy.

In conclusion, I will try to do the best I can, and study as well as I can. I know that studying in college will be hard, but I know this college will give me facility to make me grow my knowledge in there. Therefore, I know that this is the place that will give me knowledge and build me the best employee; also, the best man to survive in the world. I will expect to be qualified in your college and work in your team.

Student E, final paragraph of recommendation paper; second-semester non-native composition course

Advantages in nanotechnology have the potential to completely update many aspects of medicine and health care, includes developing very rapid gene sequencing devices, and it will make each individual therapy possible. Efficient drug discovery and new way of delivering medicine into human body, other than having benefit on medicine and health care, nanotechnology will also has the significant impacts on energy efficiency, it can be used to supervise and fix environmental problem. Such as saving the energy that wasting on all the industry, and reducing the pollution. In a way of preventing pollution by the development of nanotechnology, they're also an unfriendly affect on the environment. Nanotechnology has negative potentials that could cause ecological disaster if they go unregulated, but it is not too late to exercise the control. The most concern that the nanotechnology brings is not yet the environmental impaction. September 11th certainly has made us clearly understand the impact that terrorists can bring, small group of people can cause of thousands of people to the end of their life, with the nanotechnoloy new weapon could definitely be much powerful than what we have currently, and if the terrorists is also appear in the time that the nanotechnology weapon already produced, how many people can be killed by just tiny group of people? Well, again, it is not too late to prevent negative impact on the nanotechnoloy, what will happen is depended on what we do and how we do today. Cautiously concern with the negative impact and take every advantage of the nanotechnology that benefit our society, together to make a better tomorrow.

Punctuation:
Another Foreign Language

ENGLISH PUNCTUATION.

CHAPTER I.
INTRODUCTION.

SECT. I.—THE IMPORTANCE AND USES OF CORRECT
PUNCTUATION.

No one will hesitate to admit, that next in value to the capacity of discerning or discovering truth, and of feeling the blessed relations which we sustain to the Being who made us, and to our fellow-creatures, particularly those with whom we are more immediately connected, is the power by which intelligence and emotion are communicated from one mind to another. By it the great and gifted of past times have bequeathed to us many a rich legacy of thought and deed ; and by it those of the present either re-create the old materials, or fashion new ones, for the delight and improvement of their own generation ; and transmit to the future, — to beings yet unborn, — their treasures of wisdom, of genius, and of love. This power, it is needless to say, is language, oral and written, especially the latter.

But, as oral speech has its tones and inflections, its pauses and its emphases, and other variations of voice, to give greater expression to the thoughts which spoken words represent, and to produce on the mind of the hearer a more rapid and intense impression than lifeless enunciation could effect ; so written or printed language is usually accompanied by marks or points, to enable the reader to comprehend at a glance the precise and determinate sense of the author, — a sense which, without these marks, would in many instances be gathered only by an elaborate and painful process, and very often be misunderstood. It therefore obviously follows, that the art which serves to elucidate the meaning of a writer, to bring out his ideas with more facility, and to render his expressions a genuine transcript of the feelings and sentiments which he would convey to the hearts and the minds of others, is entitled to no small degree of attention.

Now, it is indisputable that Punctuation *does* conduce to make written language more effective, by exhibiting with greater precision and definiteness the ideas, feelings, and emotions of an author, than could be accomplished by a mass of words, however well chosen, if brought together without those peculiar marks which show the multifarious varieties of union or of separation existing in thought and expression. For what is Punctuation, and what its aim? It is the art of dividing a literary composition into sentences, by means of points, for the purpose of exhibiting the various combinations, connections, and dependencies of words. And what is this process but a means of facilitating that analysis and combination which must be made, consciously or unconsciously, before we can penetrate to the very core of an author's thoughts, and appropriate them as food for the life and growth of our own minds?

—John Wilson, 1856, *A Treatise on English Punctuation*
(Boston: Crosby, Nichols, and Company)

This passage is an excerpt from a book by John Wilson published in Boston in 1856 on the uses and forms of English punctuation. Because it introduces major assumptions about the role of punctuation symbols, it is a useful place to begin this chapter on the challenges that punctuation—and design elements more generally—pose for second language writers. Wilson suggests that punctuation serves to "enable the reader to comprehend at a glance the precise and determinate sense of the author" and to "[divide] a literary composition into sentences, by means of points, for the purpose of exhibiting the various combinations, connections, and dependencies of words." In short, it serves as a tool for adding both inflection and segmentation to written text.

In addition to the passage's content, however, the excerpt also provides a graphic illustration of the difficulties second language writers are likely to encounter when attempting to master current conventions for English punctuation, layout, and design. Imagine for a moment that the majority of texts you had read for the past twelve years followed the conventions in Wilson's book. You might assume that periods were used at the ends of what you know to be a sentence but also at the ends of titles and section headers. You would assume that semi-colons function to segment sentences that are getting too long and that they should be written with a space before and after them. You would assume that initial paragraphs should not be marked by an indent but that all subsequent paragraphs should be and that as with Wilson's second paragraph it is perfectly acceptable for the sentences in the paragraph to be so long that an argument can be made, developed, and concluded in only two sentences. You would assume that if a topic is in focus or the topic of the discussion, then that is sufficient reason to capitalize it, as *Punctuation* is in this example. You would also accept liberal policies for capitalizing references to deities and the use of italics as a marker of verbal emphasis (cf., *does*). Finally, it is important to realize that you would primarily have learned these conventions through examples, until you read Wilson's book.

If the conventions for English have changed this much in a little more than 150 years, imagine the variability that students crossing languages may encounter. Conventions for punctuation, layout, and design are not based in inherent or universal notions of what makes a text easier to read, and so the hypotheses that students bring to English about what such devices symbolize may also vary widely. Students' first languages may or may not use the same range of symbols and graphic conventions as English; the symbols may be used for different purposes or with different frequencies; text may or may not flow in the same direction across the page; and most important, the same degree of standardization that exists for academic English may simply not exist. The significance of these cross-linguistic differences will vary depending on the language but, at the very least, the differences mean that students cannot confidently transfer into English the conventions of their first language.

This problem is compounded by a tendency for both English language and composition classes to treat punctuation and design as only marginally related to their core goals. Guidelines for using different symbols and layout features can be found in handbooks, but they are rarely the focus of explicit instruction. There may be some attention paid in a class to periods and commas and possibly semi-colons, but it is highly unlikely that markers such as colons, hyphens, dashes, ellipses, brackets, or italics will be discussed. Moreover, if we think about the two functions that Wilson lists for punctuation—inflection and segmentation—teachers are much more likely to focus on the marking of syntactic boundaries than ways to add rhythm, emphasis, or hierarchy to a text. When it comes to formatting a paper, university instructors often assume that they do not need to specify guidelines or that they can simply direct students toward a particular publication or style manual. If you think about the size and level of detail in most handbooks and publication manuals, however, you may realize how overwhelming the instruction to go teach yourself can be for second language writers.

Variable exposure compounded by limited instruction may impact students in two ways. First, it may mean that they do not know how to use a device appropriately or even that the device exists. This is the problem that handbooks and to some extent publication manuals are designed to address. Handbooks are generally produced by commercial publishers and serve as reference guides providing focused explanations of everything from composing strategies to grammatical terminology to conventional usages for different punctuation devices. Publication manuals such as those produced by the Modern Language Association (MLA) and the American Psychological Association (APA) tend to focus more on issues related to formatting papers and the citation of references. The second problem students face occurs when they do not realize how important the devices can be for a reader. On many occasions I have been told by students that they were never taught any rules for punctuating either their first language or their second. As a result, they naturally assumed that punctuation was not really a major issue, but we all know it can be.

The excerpt on pages 117–18 is the beginning of a student paper comparing two positions on the impact of CO_2 emissions on climate change. The positions had been introduced through course readings, and I had supplied the student with guidelines for typing the paper. The guidelines called for following the *Publication Manual of the American Psychological Association* (5th edition); using 11 or 12 point type throughout; and including a header that listed student name, course number, assignment name, and due date on the first page and student last name plus page number on the subsequent pages. I had not suggested a handbook or given the students any help with punctuation.

Unity in our opposition

Pseudo science one of the main descriptions associated with climate change study ,it 's a common believe since a majority of people can't view climate change study in full dimensions ,as in , they don't consider the great analysis , research and lab skill required in this field . There believe comes utterly from their thinking that scientists in climate change write about obvious things and can't agree on it, to them it's just a temperature and humidity variation nothing hard to interpret. the critical question is how can we make them understand that climate change is much deeper than that and convince and even make them to believe that we are facing a climate crisis now ,although we don't seem to agree on anything regarding it .the challenge here that how can we deliver that message efficiently. We can't just simply tell them look around you because they can't see problem in their surrounds ; they are probably having a nice house ,sitting in a comfortable coach reading this essay about climate change it 's inconvenient to be honest. And even if they did look around ,since we disagree which way they should look and who they should believe ,therefore, it 's easier for them to neglect the existence of the problem. why we should care about those old fashion, stubborn people and probably uneducated individuals who can't realize that we are heading to a cliff when it's pretty clear ;"Why??"the answer basically is because saving our plant is a mission that requires us all ,moreover, those people do represent a decent ,affecting population .We can deal with them by confronting them with their arguments and prove that our opposition when it comes to the problem of climate change is really an evidence that support us and force or the as preferred encourage people to work toward the solution of the problem . A sample of our apposition is a group of articles .We are going view their authors contrasting opinions regarding the CO_2 relation with climate change to reach a point unity at least in the sense of realizing the problem .the article are .First we have "Chain is growing CO_2 emissions" for" Glen P. Peters" ,who conceives the increase in CO_2 emissions as the main factor of climate change in china .which is a consequence of the increase in production and economic development that results in the increase of energy consumption as well .Secondly ,the two

> articles of Phillip Sttot who considered CO_2 a secondary factor .In
> "You can't control the climate " article he suggests that cosmic ray
> activity is the main cause of "Global warming" not CO_2 .his
> approach in the second article "Power poverty and climate
> colonialism " shows that he is concerned more the global issue of
> the enforce of authority of developed country on development
> countries and how developed countries want to impose a reduction
> in energy consumption of development countries that barely have it
> , ignoring their own stand in the situation ,Inaddition, knowing that
> they are the cause of the problem. The intersection between the two
> opposite point of views will mean a confirmed result and will initiate
> a reaction coming from belief towards our problem

This is only the first paragraph, but the rest of the paper continues in the same vein. From a rhetorical perspective the paper accomplished many of the goals I had set in class for the assignment. In particular, it establishes a problem for the reader that could be addressed by comparing different authors' views. I did not realize this the first time I read the paper, however.

I was too overwhelmed by issues of punctuation and formatting (not to mention syntax and spelling). The position of spaces relative to periods, commas, semi-colons, apostrophes, and quotation marks varies throughout the essay. Capitalization of proper nouns like China is also inconsistent. Periods are used where I would not use them and vice versa. The question mark after *Why* is doubled, possibly in an attempt to add emphasis, and the whole expression is put in quotation marks even though it functions as a rhetorical question posed by the writer. The first line of the paragraph is not indented (nor is the first line of any of the subsequent paragraphs). And finally the header for every page contained the student's full name followed by the student's major and year of graduation. In short, the issues are numerous, and they impede my ability to focus on the message of the text—a definite sign that intervention is needed.

When students are taught punctuation, it is usually via lists with titles such as Uses for the Comma or Where to Put a Semi-Colon. If we think about it, however, this is probably a backward approach to meeting their needs. A student who is writing a paper is faced with two questions. First, do I need something here? Then, if so, what do I need? The place to start, therefore, seems to be with the roles that punctuation, graphic elements, and layout features play in shaping a written message. Once a need has been recognized, students need knowledge of the choices for addressing it. What follows is a series of functional roles that may be filled by punctuation and design elements. They are organized according to the broad categories of segmentation and inflection that we saw introduced in Wilson's work. As with much of the material in this book, the goal is to provide a framework for talking about the issue when it arises rather than a comprehensive list of everything students need to know before they begin writing.

Segmentation

Spoken language often strings together a wide range of syntactic constructions. Sentences that start but never finish, verbs with no subjects, and one-word phrases frequently flow one after the other. To make matters even more difficult, the language comes out almost as a steady stream of sound with nothing equivalent to the white space between words on a printed page to help the listener comprehend what is being said. But at some point, speakers stop, maybe just for a few milliseconds. This brief pause serves a very important function. It signals to the listener that the stream that has just emerged should be interpreted as an informational unit—regardless of its grammatical properties. In effect, it tells the listener, "Now, it's your turn to figure this out."

Written language is much more standardized than spoken language in terms of acceptable syntactic constructions, but it also frequently packs in a lot more information. We are much more likely to find extensive modification, use of **subordination,** and more specialized vocabulary in written language than spoken.

Thus, readers too benefit from signals that say, "Treat this segment as a chunk of information." With written language, however, the system goes beyond simply segmenting chunks; it also characterizes the nature or status of the chunk and the information it represents. The characterizations may signal that a unit should be interpreted as a whole or as a component part. They may also signal whether the unit is an argument or a marker of authorship or explanatory text. The next discussion divides the systematic use of punctuation and graphic features into two levels: a local level that segments the flow of text, much like pauses in spoken language, and then a more global level that serves to segment and characterize larger, more complex chunks of text.

Local

Written text flows in the form of major units (sentences) comprised of more minor units (clauses). From a syntactic point of view, sentences are usually defined as an independent clause and all associated dependent clauses (cf., Chapter 6). Under certain conditions, two independent clauses (or even occasionally a series of independent clauses) and their related dependent clauses may be joined together. It is also possible, however, for a writer to elevate a single word or phrase to the status of a sentence by punctuating it as such. That writers would want to elevate phrases in this way indicates that sentences also have semantic associations with notions such as completeness, significance, and apartness and that it is possible to use punctuation to move informational units up or down a semantic continuum of distinctness. The devices used to mark these local boundaries include what are conventionally thought of as punctuation marks (periods, questions marks, exclamation marks, commas, semi-colons, and colons) as well as dashes, parentheses, bullets, and numbering. In discussing punctuation with a second language writer, three levels of local boundaries can be recognized, each corresponding to a different degree of distinctness.

- **High-level boundaries.** The boundary that marks the greatest distinction between two units occurs between two sentences. Such boundaries are marked by periods, question marks, and exclamation marks followed by the capitalization of the first letter of the succeeding word. These marks signal the end of a unit that has a stand-alone quality and that can frequently be interpreted as making a unique contribution to the overall meaning of the text. It may be a statement of an argument, a statement of an example, or an evaluation of a proposition made in another sentence. As noted, the default syntax for this type of unit is an independent clause with any associated dependent clauses. The choice between the three marks depends on whether the sentence is a declarative statement, a question (rhetorical or real), or an emphatic utterance. It should be noted that the choice between a declarative statement marked by a period and an emphatic utterance marked by an exclamation mark often relates to the type of writing and whether exclamations are considered appropriate. Capitalization may also be a problem for students if the majority of their writing has used a script which does not have paired upper and lower case symbols.

- **Mid-level boundaries.** In the middle of the continuum are boundaries that instead of signaling a clear break indicate what we might call a *linked* break. This kind of break is marked either by a comma plus a coordinating conjunction (*and, but, for, or, nor, yet, so*) or a semi-colon. Typically the two units could be stand-alone sentences, but they share some type of logical or dependent relation that the writer wishes to make explicit. The comma is used with a closed set of conjunctions that learners may need to memorize; the semi-colon may be used with or without a wider set of transitional words (cf., the present sentence). One current convention for English that may need to be shared is that normally we do not link more than two units in this fashion.

Some languages such as Arabic use coordinating conjunctions as a type of lexical period and may string large sections of text together using equivalents to *and* or *so*. This is comprehensible for a reader of English, but it goes against the convention.

- **Low-level boundaries**. Finally, there are boundaries that interrupt the flow of the sentence, often as a way of indicating an explanatory or evaluative aside. Handbooks are filled with suggested uses for commas, dashes, colons, and parentheses that fit into this broad category, but here are a few of the more common types with examples from this chapter and Chapter 1:

1. Commas setting aside a phrase or clause that comes at the beginning or in the middle of the sentence and that modifies the rest of the sentence (note that the set apart expression often serves as a transition linking the sentence to the rest of the text).

   > In addition to the passage's **content, however, the** excerpt also provides a graphic illustration of the difficulties second language writers are likely to encounter when attempting to master current conventions for English punctuation, layout, and design.

   > **Finally, there** are boundaries that interrupt the flow of the sentence, often as a way of indicating an explanatory or evaluative aside.

2. Commas or dashes setting aside a phrase or clause that functions like a side comment.

   > With top-down strategies we focus on the overall **meaning, building** an evolving model for the message of the text that we then use to figure out new pieces of the puzzle.

*The following discussion divides the systematic use of punctuation and graphic features into two levels: a local level which segments the flow of **text, much like pauses in spoken language, and** then a more global level that serves to segment and characterize larger, more complex chunks of text.*

*Because it introduces major assumptions about the role of punctuation symbols, it is a useful place to begin this chapter on the challenges that **punctuation—and design elements more generally—pose** for second language writers.*

*Finally, it is important to realize that you would primarily have learned these conventions through **examples—until** you read Wilson's book.*

3. Commas setting aside a non-restrictive adjectival dependent clause (i.e., one that has the syntactic form of an adjective clause but that comments on the noun being modified instead of specifying or otherwise limiting it).

   *The problem with bottom-up reading at this point, however, is that it distracts you from your **job, which** is to devise a plan for helping Ming improve the essay as a whole and become a better writer in general.*

4. Commas, dashes, parentheses, or colons setting apart appositives (i.e., phrases that rename or restate a concept that has just been introduced) or constructions that are syntactically parallel but not necessarily semantically equivalent.

   *The more you **read, the** more confused you become.*

   The following discussion divides the systematic use of punctuation and graphic features into two levels: a local level which segments the flow of text, much like pauses in spoken language, and then a more global level that serves to segment and characterize larger, more complex chunks of text.

*Finally, there is one special type of low-level **boundary, the series, which** consists of three or more syntactically parallel units.*

*Reading researchers generally talk about two complementary strategies for deciphering a **text: top-down** and bottom-up.*

5. Commas, numbers, or bullets indicating the elements in a series (note that the beginning of a series is sometimes marked by a colon as in this set of examples).

   *You would assume that initial paragraphs should not be marked by an indent but that all subsequent paragraphs should be and that as with Wilson's second paragraph it is perfectly acceptable for the sentences in the paragraph to be so long that an argument can be **made, developed, and concluded** in only two sentences.*

As an illustration of these three levels of local boundaries, consider the excerpt on page 125 from the student's essay. The original punctuation has been removed, and the bracketed words have been inserted to help with readability. Rather than insert conventional punctuation, however, I have simply indicated whether I believe current conventions would mark a boundary as low (/), mid (//), or high (///) level.

pseudo-science [is] one of the main descriptions associated with climate change study /// it's a common [belief] since a majority of people can't view climate change study in full dimensions / as in they don't consider the great analysis / research / and lab skill required in this field /// there [belief] comes utterly from their thinking that scientists in climate change write about obvious things and can't agree on it // to them it's just a temperature and humidity variation / nothing hard to interpret /// the critical question is how can we make them understand that climate change is much deeper than that and convince and even make them to believe that we are facing a climate crisis now / although we don't seem to agree on anything regarding it ///

Tutoring / Teaching Tip

If students have significant problems figuring out when to segment the flow of text, it may be helpful to take a paragraph they have written, remove all the punctuation (including capitalization), and then ask them to punctuate it in a stepwise fashion. First, they should draw a single line to indicate where boundaries are needed. Then ask them to decide which of those boundaries should be mid-level and which high-level boundaries, in which case they can add additional break lines. Finally, for each break, they should choose the best device for marking the break. As part of this exercise, they may learn a lot from hearing you explain why you would or would not break at a certain location.

Global

In contrast to local segments, which are identified based on their internal syntactic and informational characteristics, global segments derive their identity from their function in the text as a whole. For example, we can divide a text into paragraphs and hierarchically organized sections. We also recognize different component parts such as the title, abstract, header, or reference list. We may even go so far as to graphically mark discourse units such as arguments, key points, introductions, or conclusions. The conventions for marking global segments tend to be more variable than those for local segments. Thus paragraphs may be marked by indenting the first line or leaving more white space between two lines than normal. A text that is divided into sections typically employs headers, but the headers may be marked with a numbered hierarchy (e.g., 1, 1.1, 1.2, 2, 2.1.1) or changes in font effects (type, size, underlining, etc.). Titles are frequently centered but not always. They may also employ a different or larger font or even appear on a separate page. Key points may be bolded as part of the regular text or repeated in graphic call outs.

The full range of units and possibilities for marking them are beyond the scope of this book. We must be prepared, however, to help students understand that such conventions exist, identify the relevant segments of their text, and develop strategies for figuring out which conventions they should follow. In academic contexts, faculty often dictate a particular style manual (e.g., *The MLA Handbook*) for use in preparing written assignments. These provide evidence that conventions exist, but which segments are actually needed depends on the particular type of writing. Many style manuals include separate guidelines for class assignments, theses, and academic journal submissions. Rather than simply telling students what segments should be included, it may be more helpful to provide them with example papers and ask them to identify the sections. This can be especially helpful if you are working on headers that mark different levels of a text since many second language learners may not realize the significance of levels when they read either.

Finally, you want to make sure students understand that at a very general level, the function of these global markers is to make it easier for a reader to find information in a text. They should understand that readers typically want to process a text as fast as possible, that they may or may not read from beginning to end, and that key information should be salient. Systems for marking textual divisions therefore typically rely on consistency (marking similar units in similar ways) and hierarchy (making some units more prominently than others). Thus the header on the first page of a class paper typically contains more information than the header on subsequent pages. The function of the first page header is to link the paper to the collected works of the student; whereas, the subsequent headers need only to order the pages with respect to the first page. Likewise, section headers are typically more complex than basic divisions between paragraphs.

One unit of writing that may be particularly problematic for students is the paragraph. Paragraphs are frequently taught as having a very formal structure beginning with a topic sentence, followed by sentences that develop the topic and sentences that support the claims made while developing the topic. Clearly there should be a topical unity to a paragraph, but figuring out when to begin or end a new paragraph is not necessarily intuitive. There is no rule for how long or how short a paragraph should be. I think it can be instructive for students to look at sample texts, especially ones written by other students, and simply notice how much space paragraphs typically take up on a page. Paragraphs in contemporary academic English rarely take up more than a whole page, but they are usually longer than four lines. It may also be helpful for students to think of the paragraph as a signal to a reader that if you must take a break, here is a good place to do so. In other words, instead of trying to define the paragraph in terms of its components as we would if it were a local segment, treat it as a global segment and focus on its role in making the text more readable.

Tutoring / Teaching Tip

One way of introducing the function and value of global segment markers is to show students a text from a language that they do not know. Ask them what hypotheses they can make about where textual divisions lie and how different segments function. You can also ask them to describe what purpose the text as a whole serves. See what inferences they can make based on formatting and layout. Similarly, you may want to show them two pages from different types of English texts (e.g., a magazine article and an academic journal article or a class paper and an academic journal article) and ask them what kind of writing the pages came from. Both of these exercises direct attention to the non-verbal cues and their functions.

Inflection

The second major function for punctuation and graphic features is what I refer to as **inflection**. When describing spoken language, inflection refers to modulations of pitch and tone that indicate a layer of meaning over and above that conveyed by the words themselves, meanings such as excitement, questioning, and deliberateness. For me, inflection corresponds to what Wilson meant when he wrote that punctuation serves to "enable the reader to comprehend at a glance the precise and determinate sense of the author." Another way of thinking about this functional usage of punctuation is as a type of meta-message, an indication of how the writer wants the unit to be interpreted. The next discussion lists four types of written inflection: emphasis, attribution, abbreviation, and enhancement.

Emphasis

Writers use font formatting (bold, italics, underline), quotation marks (i.e., scare quotes), and sometimes special symbols such as an asterisk (*) or pound (#) to signal that an expression deserves special notice. They may want to emphasize the expression because it is unexpected and they are afraid the reader might skip over it. Conversely, if the expression is an argument, they may want to indicate how strongly they feel about it. Or they may simply want the reader to know that they are aware that this expression belongs to a different register. Since all of the devices for indicating emphasis may be used for other purposes as well, it is important that students avoid any possibility of ambiguity (e.g., they should not use italics to mark book titles and for emphasis in the same piece). They also need to learn the degree to which it is acceptable to emphasize expressions in their target genre. Many academic genres use emphatic expressions sparingly and often restrict them to sections where the author's opinions are more likely to appear such as the introduction or conclusion.

Attribution

One of the more complex inflection systems is that for attributing words or ideas to an outside source. The mechanics of when to attribute a source are treated in Chapter 3, but how to do that can be just as problematic for students. Students may have seen examples of both single and double quotation marks and not be certain of the difference. Variations in citation styles can also cause difficulties. Many students who are still learning attribution systems will simply put anything related to a source—the author's full name, a partial title, or the publication year by itself—in parentheses somewhere in the vicinity of a quote. They may also try to insert a hyperlink to the homepage for a site with no indication of which page on the site the material actually came from. They will not add citations for information that is not a direct quotation, and they also will not put a bibliography at the end, thinking that an in-text reference satisfies the need to signal "ownership." While it is tempting just to show the students what they need to include, this may not help them learn what they need for the next assignment, especially if the next professor requires a different citation style.

A more productive tactic may be to work on using a style manual. Help them understand the different components of an attribution system—the frame sentence for a quotation *(Smith argues that ". . .")*, the parenthetical marker that needs to be placed somewhere *(1982, p. 35)*, and then a more complete entry for the source in a note and/or bibliography. Point out that sometimes multiple sources are cited for a single piece of information, in which case they need to know how to concatenate and sequence the references. They should also note whether page numbers are used for anything other than direct quotations. Frequently they will need help with the conventions for referring to authors, especially the usage of given and family names. Finally, attribution is increasingly being facilitated by reference management software programs such as EndNote®, ProCite®, and Zotero that create a database of sources and templates for writing papers according to specific style guides. Introduce students to this technology.

Abbreviation

Yet another type of inflectional message is a signal that an expression has been abbreviated. Printed text employs a range of symbols that stand in for more complex verbal expressions. Many of these symbols (*1,2,3*, *$*, %, &, . . .) are located on the top row of a keyboard. Others include: apostrophes for contractions, ellipsis to show that words have been omitted, and shortened versions of stock Latin phrases (*etc.*, *e.g.*, *i.e.*, *et al.*). Language learners need to learn both what these symbols mean and also when it is acceptable to use them. For example, some style guides advocate spelling out the Latin abbreviations with English expressions such as *furthermore, for example*, and *specifically*. The standard advice for formal writing is also to avoid contractions and spell out numbers up to ten. Learners need to realize that using abbreviated forms is associated with less formal styles of writing.

> ## Tutoring / Teaching Tip
>
> The devices that signal inflectional meanings are much more variable than those used for segmentation. They vary with respect to genre and, if one is specified, style manual. It is therefore difficult to give students generic rules for their use. A better approach may be to try to raise student awareness using model texts. Ask students what function different devices serve. You may find that students have only a very general interpretation. I have found, for example, that if I ask students what the number after a name in a parenthetical reference signifies, they do not always realize that it is a page number. You can also approach this by asking students to rewrite a text so that it "looks like" it belongs to a different genre. This will get them to focus on the visual conventions associated with genres.

Enhancement

The final set of inflection devices play off the main stream of text by adding enhancements to it. By using devices such as footnotes, endnotes, and sidebar notes, writers resolve potential ambiguities and elaborate on tangential topics; through visual graphics they provide complementary and supplemental information that would be difficult to put into words. Again, the range of acceptable enhancement techniques varies greatly with respect to genre. Class papers rarely use footnotes or endnotes for anything other than attribution, although there are disciplines (e.g., English literature) that use them extensively for adding supplemental information. Graphs and figures, on the other hand, almost never occur in essay papers but are quite common in research reports. In working with learners, it is important to stress that the devices should truly enhance meaning, and not just serve as a type of window dressing filling up space on a page. You may also need to work with learners on effective titles and captions for pictures, figures, and graphs.

A Principled Approach

As previously noted, language and composition classes only rarely address punctuation and, even less, the use of graphic devices. The assumption seems to be that students will pick up appropriate usage through exposure. This is probably an unrealistic assumption for second language learners who are frequently struggling to comprehend the basic message of a text and so have much less mental attention available for how the text is printed. It is also true, however, that the complexity and variability of punctuation systems makes them difficult to teach in the abstract. If we try to prepare students for every situation where they might use a comma or all the different ways to indicate a series, there will be little time left to consider what makes an argument effective or productive processes for writing.

What can be shared with students, especially in one-on-one interaction around a specific text, is a set of principles for acquiring and using punctuation systems:

1. **Pay attention.** Punctuation and graphic features make a text more readable and its message more intelligible and/or richer. They cannot be ignored.
2. **Research the options.** Which device should be used for a particular function varies with respect to genre, formality, and possibly a prescribed style manual. It is therefore essen-

tial to research what is most acceptable and common for a given genre. Students should be encouraged to note what is not present as well as what is.

3. **Be consistent.** Punctuation and graphic features operate as parts of systems. For example, the choice of a period over a semi-colon must always indicate a complete break as opposed to a linked break. Similarly, if a first-level header is bolded and a second-level header is italicized, then this must be true for every case of each. Once the option has been chosen, stick to it.

These principles will not fix the student's essay on pages 117–18, but they will provide a framework for discussing the essay, for moving from why it needs improvement to how to figure out what to do.

Strategic One on One

When Ming came to you and handed you her paper, your biggest concern was probably, "What can I say or do in 15, 20, or even 30 minutes that will help her with this paper?" The overall goal of this book has been to introduce a body of knowledge about second language writers, their writing, and their readers that will help you come up with the particular answers that you need for working with Ming and students like her. Thus, we have seen how it helps to understand Ming as a person and as a language learner influenced by her previous schooling and her social circumstances. We have seen that before we can work on a paper, we must understand what the paper is expected to accomplish, both from the standpoint of the teacher who assigned it and the readers for whom it is intended. We also have to understand how language coalesces into written text and then the varying conventions for presenting that text. Beyond the particular answers, however, we also need strategies for presenting them to Ming. We need to realize that our opportunity to work with Ming is in fact a unique educational setting—a one-on-one interaction—and that teaching and learning in this setting is different from what happens in classrooms and through textbooks.

In contrast to these more predictable educational settings, one-on-one interactions are not scripted. We enter them without a set of learning objectives articulated with course goals or even a lesson plan for how to structure the interaction. Students also are likely to see them from a very utilitarian perspective; they simply want to improve their papers so that they can get a better grade on them. They do not see the interaction in the context of an overall course or as an opportunity to improve their literacy skills. Because of this, neither they nor we generally consider our strategies for maximizing the effectiveness of one-on-one interactions and for using them to influence more than just an immediate paper. But we should think of them as more than a chance to fix something. As a way of concluding our search for answers to give Ming, Chapter 8 introduces seven strategies for using one-on-one interactions to promote sustainable learning and make our 15 minutes matter in the long-term.

1. Identify the priorities, and let the rest slide.

Many of us are perfectionists when it comes to writing. We cannot see a missing comma or a misspelled word or a popular saying that is not quite right. We fret when students use in-text citations only for direct quotations or when they explain in detail a concept that we think a six-year-old would know. And we feel like we are doing a disservice to students if we do not mention these things. As has been noted several times, however, if we address every issue in a paper we risk overwhelming students. They may react by changing only the surface errors because those are easiest; they may also feel that all is hopeless and change nothing.

The advice instead has been to prioritize, **to decide in the context of this assignment with this learner,** what will have the greatest impact on the paper's effectiveness. Not only will this approach have a better chance of suggesting to learners steps that they can actually implement, it also teaches them about a good writing process. It shows that revision is a multi-stage process, that we should work on the

Tutoring / Teaching Tip

The priority list will be different for each writer and each piece of writing. In general, however, start with issues related to the purpose of the writing and the student's understanding of his or her audience. These issues motivate discussions about organization and flow. Next, look for issues that make it difficult to understand meaning at a particular point in the text. Finally, work on issues that may annoy you or affect your overall impressions but that do not prevent you from understanding the student's intentions.

clarity of our position and the strategies for supporting and developing it first and then examine issues of syntax and punctuation. If time permits, you may want to suggest that once they address the priority issues, they should come back so that you can discuss other issues. If time does not permit, you may want to at least make sure they understand that you have tried to indicate priority issues, not all issues. In short, make it explicit that the help you are providing should be part of an on-going process.

2. Ask students to verbalize what they are trying to do and what they hear you saying.

When you work in a second language, you learn to live with ambiguity. There will always be a certain percentage of words you hear but do not know what they mean or have only a general understanding of. You tend to focus on the gist of what is being said instead, knowing that the discussion is about a particular topic or designed to promote a particular outcome. In many cases, that is sufficient. Thus a learner may hear what you say and realize that it is a suggestion to delete. They will delete the passage and consequently improve the paper, but they may not have understood why.

Understanding why depends on their ability to talk about writing, to discuss the text in an abstract sense as a series of moves by an author trying to engage a reader. The language of these discussions is typically very abstract and often somewhat imprecise. We refer to units of discourse with unclear boundaries, asking questions like, *Why should I believe this?* or *What gets your reader's attention here?* We talk about logical relations, inferences, and implications as if they were explicitly stated in the text. And we frequently refer to the fuzzy world of affective reactions. These are the tools of the writing conference, and they cannot be avoided, but they must also be learned and practiced.

It is a useful exercise to record ourselves talking with students one on one. Often we will discover in retrospect that we thought we were having a balanced and interactive conversation when in fact we were expounding and students were simply signaling that they understood. Their contribution was to say *yes* or *um-hmm* and then occasionally to ask a one-word question like *why?* or *how?* If this is our conversation, then we have practiced the abstract language for talking about writing, and our students have been passive listeners focusing on the gist. As part of conferencing, therefore, we need to ask students both to verbalize their strategies and abstract motivations with respect to the text and also to repeat back to us what they hear us saying. By practicing the meta-language for writing, students develop their ability to seek and understand input and, more important, to think about writing without ambiguity.

3. Model the reader.

When we talk about writing, we are talking as a teacher. We are trying to develop students' expertise in the content knowledge of composition and rhetorical studies. But one-on-one interactions should do more than build expertise; they should also develop students' ability to practice their expertise, to craft effective messages. Thus, students need to learn not only how to talk about crafting but also how to gauge their product's effectiveness.

In order for a message to be effective, it must achieve a desired result with an audience. In a conversation the audience is in front of us, we can sense when they are bored or puzzled or excited by simply looking at their face. Writers do not have this luxury, and developing writers (both first and second language) typically have a hard time thinking about how readers will react to their writing. They assume omniscient knowledge of referents, causes, and goals. They think through a process before they write, and then commit to paper only the beginning and end. They state something that for them has an obvious implication and proceed as if the implication has been explicitly stated. If they are a second language writer, they may simply not know what their audience will or will not know.

Thus in addition to helping students learn to verbalize what is happening in a text, one-on-one interactions can also help them to visualize what will happen when the text is actually read. We can preface our comments with qualifiers like, "As I'm reading this, I'm thinking . . . " or "When I read this word, it reminds me of . . . " We may also want to sequence the conference according to the way that a first-time reader is likely to approach the text. In doing this, remember that not all texts are processed from beginning to end. Readers of some types of technical documents in particular are likely to read the introduction, and then jump to the conclusions before deciding if they want to find out about the exact methods and procedures. We may also want to talk about the impressions we bring to a text that are based on past experiences. For example, we can make comments like, "When I read research reports, I often check the bibliography first." One-on-one conferences provide an excellent way to model the one-on-one conversations that happen between a writer and a reader via a text.

4. Talk about texts as sites of strategic interaction.

One of the difficulties that students face when envisioning readers is that they often do not think of their writing as something that has a functional purpose or goal. Inside academia we write because we are told to; outside academia we write because we want to satisfy a need or achieve a goal. If the stakes for a report or a proposal are high, then we think a lot about what will really convince our audience, how much information they need as background, and where to slip in the explanation for why our costs are higher than a competitor's. Student writers, on the other hand, often think more in terms of the content that needs to go in the paper. They focus on how many sources or reasons they should include, whether they can make a specific claim, and what is left to say in the conclusion.

If students are asking these questions, it is in part because they do not have an independent way of evaluating the answers. The number of sources for them depends solely on how many the instructor wants. Whether they can make a claim depends on whether the instructor says it is acceptable to include their opinion. The students are correct that in academic writing, the instructor's opinion is all that really matters. Thinking about the instructor's response as totally arbitrary, however, is not helpful. In one-on-one conferences, we can direct students toward a more productive understanding of the motivating forces behind a text, if we prompt them to think strategically. Their goal should be to impress their instructor, not satisfy his or her whims. If we can therefore help them to see their texts as a series of strategic moves, which function both to set up subsequent moves and to bring in qualities that are likely to impress, we give them a scale on which to judge their own writing and prepare them for their future writing outside of the academy.

5. Build analysis skills.

Part of impressing instructors is realizing why instructors assign writing in the first place. If the assignment is for a writing course, then the goal is usually practice in the crafting of an effective form. If it is for a non-composition course, then the instructor may also seek evidence of research abilities and awareness of disciplinary norms and practices. Across the board, however, instructors tend to see writing as an exercise that promotes thinking skills. Writing requires the invention of arguments, the marking of logical connections, and the ability to group and sequence. It is important to realize, however, that we believe it is possible to create better or worse arguments, clear or unclear connections, and groups that make sense and groups that do not make sense. In other words, thinking skills are something that we develop over time and through practice, which leads us back to the goal for assigning writing in the first place.

One-on-one interactions because of their individualized nature provide an excellent opportunity to help students improve their thinking skills. We can challenge students with counter-examples to their arguments, point out non-sequiturs, push them to extend their justifications, and identify other instances where a claim applies. We can ask them to draw visual representations of a text's organization or compare their text with another. Finally we can model these skills by taking an undeveloped idea and discussing hypothetical ways it might be developed more. To the extent that we can help students see writing as a way of creating new ideas and knowledge, we are helping them to achieve the broader goals of higher education.

6. Focus on the lesson in the particular.

When we interact around a particular paper, we feel that we are teaching something that truly matters, something that we know will be useful to the student. In focusing on an immediate issue, however, we need to keep in mind that academic writing assignments are usually not ends in themselves; they are part of this larger educational process. Thus, if we help a student improve a paper without linking that help to a broader understanding of reader expectations, community conventions, and syntactic patterns, we have subverted the curricular goals of the assignment.

We also need to be careful not to assume that students will naturally make the connection. We may tell a student that we have expectations based on the first sentence of a paragraph that are not met by the second. We may even suggest a change to one or the other sentence. We cannot assume, however, that students will learn from this to ask themselves what a reader, who does not know the master plan for the essay, is thinking as they read in real time. Nor, can we assume that they will realize that readers tend to make predictions based on archetypal organizational patterns. The ability to abstract lessons and principles from particular experiences and to draw connections between experiences is also something that students develop as they progress through their education. We can encourage this process during our one-on-one time by asking them to state explicitly what they have learned that will help them in the future. Encourage them to talk explicitly about next time. You may even want to ask them what they would do if they were writing something like this as part of a job.

7. Build independence.

The ultimate goal of the one-on-one interaction is to help students move beyond being "students." We encourage them to talk with us about their writing in the first place because we realize that they need help managing the writing process, envisioning their readers, and creating content. In the process of talking through a text, we know that strategies become more honed and deficiencies more apparent. Talking also puts meat on unstated and undeveloped principles and provides opportunities to fill in gaps. But in the end, we want students to be able to do these things by themselves.

We want them to manage the process instead of us. Students should continue to seek input, but we want them to go to their peers and already know what questions they should ask about their writing. When they are writing a paper in graduate school, we want them to realize that a style manual will dictate how to format a particular element and to be able to find that information in the manual. If they hope that their conference proposal will be accepted, we want them to expect that they can find guides about well-written proposals by searching writing center websites on the Internet. Again, we can promote this independence by asking them what they have learned about managing the process and finding answers and what they may try differently in the future. We also can let them know that sooner or later the balance of power will have to shift, and they will have to be the one working one on one.

Glossary

adjective (part of speech)—label for words that limit, modify, or describe **nouns**

adverb (part of speech)—label for words that modify or limit **verbs, adjectives,** or **clauses;** typical meanings include manner (*quickly, surreptitiously*), time (*yesterday*), location (*there*), reason (*consequently*), and degree (*many*)

agreement—relation in which the form of one word is determined by the meaning of another; in English occurs when a **verb** is marked for the number and person of the **subject** and a **pronoun** or **demonstrative** is marked for the number and proximity of its referent

aspect—grammatical property of a verb that expresses whether the action is ongoing or completed; ongoing meaning is called progressive aspect and is marked by using the *-ing* form of the verb (*they are dancing*); completed meaning is called perfective aspect and is marked by using the past participle form of the verb (*they have danced*)

clause—unit of language containing at a minimum a verb and an indicator of the verb's **subject** and any words that may be related to the subject or verb; may or may not be able to stand alone as a **sentence**

cohesion—the devices in a text that connect its different sentences and make it clear that they belong together; common devices include the use of the **definite article** (*the*), **demonstratives** (*this/that, these/those*), **pronouns, repetition** of words, and **transitional expressions**

collocation—property of words that makes them more likely to occur in the environment of some words than others; for example *painter* is more likely to occur after *house* than *shack*

conjunct—syntactic term referring to a word, phrase, or clause that links one sentence to another; **transitional expressions** are one example

definite article—*the*; generally indicates that the noun that follows has a specific referent that a reader or hearer can be assumed to understand; sometimes, however, used with generic referents as in *The camel has been a useful means of transporting goods for centuries*

demonstratives—a set of words (*this, that, these, those*) that may function either as a **pronoun** or a **determiner** and indicate whether an entity being referred to is near or far

dependent clause—type of **finite clause** that cannot be used by itself as a sentence; may serve adjectival (*The student who had stayed up all night did not wake up for class*), nominal (*What I want to know is where I put my keys*), or adverbial (*We wanted to finish dinner before the game started*) functions within a sentence

determiner—group of words that occur before nouns in English and that serve to clarify the properties or referent of the noun; include articles (*the/a book*, possessives (*my/his/our book*), numbers and quantifiers (*two books, many books*), and **demonstratives** (*this/that book*)

finite clause—**clause** for which the **tense** (present, past, future) of the verb is clear; includes both **independent** and **dependent** clauses

flow—property of a text that allows a reader to read without stopping; creating flow requires careful consideration of what the reader will and will not know as well as the information needed at any point in the text to form an interpretation

fossilized structures—word usage patterns that are different from what is commonly accepted as the standard pattern (such as using *she go* where most people expect *she goes*) and that language learners keep using even after the pattern has been explained to them; often these are patterns that do not interfere with understanding the writer's intentions

fragment—group of words punctuated as a single sentence but that most people would not accept as expressing a complete meaning; a common example with second language writers is sentences using a form of the verb *be* but that do not have a subject (*Is very dangerous when you go there.*)

Generation 1.5 students—refers to university students who immigrated to the United States while they were in elementary, middle, or high school; their educational background is therefore different from students who studied and learned English in other countries before coming to the United States for university work

genre—named category of texts such as book reports, business letters, or research papers that serve a common social and communicative purpose and that can be recognized by particular structural features

gerund—type of **non-finite clause** that serves a nominal function in a sentence; headed by the *-ing* form of a verb (*Actually seeing it amazed us all.*)

grammatical (or syntactic) meaning—category of meaning that can be applied to sets of words and is used to show relations between concepts referred to by individual words (i.e., **lexical meanings**); examples include whether a noun is definite, what the agent or instigator of a verbal action is, and that one word modifies or limits another

grammatical words—those that express properties or relations of a class of **lexical words**; typically difficult to define and often considered to exist in closed sets because of the difficulty of creating new ones; include **determiners, conjunctions,** helping/auxiliary verbs, **modals, prepositions,** and **pronouns**

indefinite article—*a/an*; indicates one instance of a noun without specifying which instance; note that it cannot be used with nouns such as *sugar* that cannot be counted; the word *some* is considered by some to be a plural form

independent clause—type of **finite clause** that can be used by itself as a sentence if desired (*We wanted to finish dinner.* / *We wanted to finish dinner* before the game started.)

infinitive—type of **non-finite clause** headed by the simple or base form of a verb usually preceded by *to* (*to walk*); may serve as a nominal (*We wanted to go home* / *To find him there* surprised us all.), adjectival (*The play to be performed tonight should be spectacular.*), or adverbial (*To access this computer,* you must know the password.); note that may include a word that functions like a subject and that the *to* is optional in some cases (*He made me (to) feel as if I were a fool.*)

inflection—(a) type of **suffix** that adds a **grammatical meaning** to a word; English inflections are *-s, -ed, -ing, -est, -er*; (b) term used in Chapter 7 to refer to author's use of punctuation and graphic elements to indicate concepts like emphasis, attribution, abbreviation, and enhancement

information order—the order in which concepts and entities are presented in a sentence; the informational units in a sentence can be sequenced in ways that make it more or less difficult to see how the sentence relates to the previous sentence

interjection (part of speech)—group of words such as *oh* or *wow* that usually bear little relation to other words in a sentence and express an emotional reaction; sometimes they are punctuated as one word sentences in writing

lexical meaning—category of meaning that can be used to distinguish one word from another; typically the explanation found in a dictionary

lexical words—words that refer to concepts, entities, actions, qualities, and relations; includes words categorized as **nouns, verbs, adjectives, adverbs**

lexis—knowledge of what words refer to, what topics and social settings they are commonly used in, and what other words they are commonly used with

lingua franca—language used for communication among people who are not native speakers of the language but who do not have another common language; English currently serves as a lingua franca for international business, and for scientific and academic communication around the world

metadiscourse—words and phrases such as *in this paper, next, as shown above*, and *in conclusion* that refer to the way a text or argument is organized or constructed; some people refer to these as a "road map for the reader"

modal—a class of **grammatical words** that indicate whether a verb is possible, likely, obligatory, permitted, or a good idea; when added to a verb they make it **finite**; English modals are *can, could, may, might, must, will, would, shall, should, ought to, have to, be going to*

non-finite clause—**clause** in which the **tense** (present, past, future) of the verb is not clear; types are **gerunds** (<u>*Growing old*</u> *is diffi-cult*), **infinitives** (*We wanted* <u>*to go home*</u>), and **participials** (<u>*Growing old*</u>*, the man was ready to go home./ The dog* <u>*found by his owner*</u> *was ready to go home.*)

noun (part of speech)—label for words that refer to entities (people, places, things) as well concepts; may be counted in many cases and can serve to motivate the action of a **verb**

part of speech—way of categorizing words according to qualities of the meaning they represent and the way they can function in a sentence; traditional categories are **noun, verb, adjective, adverb, preposition, determiner (article), interjection,** and **conjunction**

phrase—group of words that function as a single unit within the larger unit of a **clause**; categorized according to the **part of speech** of a head word (e.g., prepositional phrases, noun phrases)

positive evidence—teaching technique based on providing examples of what you want students to produce rather than explaining what is wrong with what they produced; relies on students' ability to infer patterns from examples

predicate—**clause** unit containing the **verb** and any words that complete the meaning of the verb; does not include words associated with the **subject**

prefix—unit within a **word** that precedes the **root;** serves to modify the meaning of a particular part of speech; for example, *re-* can be attached to the beginning of verbs and indicates that the verbal action expressed by the root is being done again

preposition (part of speech)—label for a class of **grammatical words** that express relations; meanings frequently have a spatial (*in, at, on, from*) or temporal (*after, during*) quality; may be used after **verbs** (*walk in*) or at the beginning of a phrase (*in the dark*); note that there are a number of multi-word prepositions (*because of, due to, in front of*)

reduced clauses—clauses that begin with a participial form of the verb (*given, giving*) and therefore omit the subject and any tense marker; dependent clauses can often be reduced without changing the meaning of a sentence (*The man who gave me the book was my father.* → *The man giving me the book was my father.*)

referential ties—words that stand in for a concept or entity introduced earlier in the text and that create a connection between the current mention and the earlier use; may be pronouns or word pairs such as *home* and *our house*

register—technical term used to describe a group of syntactic and word choices that are likely to be made in relation to a particular topic (e.g., medicine, dating, art), whether the mode of communication is oral or written, and the social relations among the people communicating (e.g., same or equal status, same or different ages); linguists argue that different academic disciplines have their own registers; similar in meaning to **style**

repetition—multiple occurrences of a word, phrase, or concept across a text that serve to connect different parts of the text

root—unit of a **word** that expresses the core **lexical meaning**; may be preceded by **prefixes** and followed by **suffixes**

run-on sentence—group of words punctuated as a single sentence but containing two or more independent clauses that have not been joined using appropriate punctuation; common examples with second language writers include a string of independent clauses joined by *and* (*She went first and then we followed her and then we all met in the café*) or cases where the object of one verb is also the subject of the next (*She really hit hard the ball was going so fast*).

segmentation—use of punctuation or graphic elements to divide a text into units for interpretation

style—term used by composition specialists to refer to aspects of a text that associate it with social functions; often indicated by word choices, grammatical complexity, and terms used for references to individuals; example uses include a *formal/informal style, an academic style, a literary style*

subject—**clause** unit headed by a **noun** or **pronoun**; the **verb** generally follows and **agrees** with it in number and person; may be the instigator/agent of the verbal action (*she threw the ball*) or the passive recipient of it (*the book fell apart, the ball was thrown by her*); note that term may refer to the single word that the verb agrees with or to an entire phrase headed by the word the verb agrees with

subordination—expression of a thought using a dependent clause as opposed to an independent clause; finite clauses (ones where the verb tense is clear) may be **independent,** meaning they can function as a sentence, or **dependent,** in which case they are attached to an independent clause in order to form a sentence

suffix—unit within a **word** that follows the **root**; may change the part of speech of the root (*nation* + *al* changes a **noun** to an **adjective**) or add a **grammatical meaning** to the word (*nation* + *s* changes a singular noun to a plural noun) in which case it is called an **inflection**

syntax—the patterns of language that allow us to identify functional roles of individual words and phrases in relation to other words and phrases; patterns derive both from the form of individual words (for example, an *s* on the end of a word may mark it as possibly a noun or possibly a verb) and their placement relative to other words and phrases (if the word with the *s* follows *the*, it must be a noun); more technical term for what is commonly referred to as *grammar*

tense—grammatical property of a **finite** verb that indicates whether the action belongs to past, present, or future time; note that tense markers may also be used to indicate non-temporal meanings such as hypotheticalness (*Were I you, I would be overjoyed.*) and relevance (*Yesterday's demonstration shows us what is likely to happen in the future.*)

tone—term used by composition specialists to refer to aspects of a text or portion of a text that signal an affective quality such as playfulness, seriousness, or foreboding

topoi—patterns first recognized by classical Greek rhetoricians for developing an argument; these patterns provided ready-made strategies for exploring and categorizing relations

transitional expressions—words or phrases such as *however, furthermore, next,* and *on the other hand* that signal the logical connection between a sentence and the preceding text

unpacking—providing a more detailed explanation; students or teachers may assume that a concept is transparent when in fact its meaning is clear only to people who have directly experienced it

verb (part of speech)—label for words that refer to states of being (*feel, seem, be, have*) and actions (*go, throw, eat, reach*); may be marked for the temporality of the action or state and also whether the action or state is on-going or complete

visa students—literally a reference to students who must obtain a visa in order to study and live in a country; they are not considered immigrants and their previous education has been outside of the country where they are currently studying

voice—term used by composition specialists to refer to aspects of a text that individualize it or reveal the author's perspective and/or sensibilities

word—a unit of language expressing a concept and that in writing can be distinguished by the convention to put a space before and after it; it may be composed of smaller units such as prefixes, roots, and suffixes and participate in larger units such as **phrases** and **clauses**

word choice—selection of appropriate words for a given text and purpose; writers frequently must choose between options such as *instructor* and *teacher* and their choice will be determined not only by the meaning of the word but also the other words and topics that each option is frequently associated with

Useful Resources

This list includes materials your writing center should consider having as resources for writing tutors, teachers, and consultants. No writing or grammar handbooks have been included here.

Journals

Journal of Second Language Writing
www.elsevier.com/locate/jslw
Journal of English for Academic Purposes
www.elsevier.com/locate/jeap
English for Specific Purposes
www.elsevier.com/locate/esp

Books and Multimedia
Article Anthologies

Second Language Writing in the Composition Classroom: A Critical Sourcebook. Eds. Paul Kei Matsuda, Michelle Cox, Jay Jordan, and Christina Ortmeier-Hooper. Boston: Bedford; Urbana, IL: NCTE, 2006.

On Second Language Writing. Eds. Tony Silva and Paul Kei Matsuda. Mahwah, NJ: Lawrence Erlbaum Associates, 2001.

Landmark Essays on ESL Writing. Eds. Tony Silva and Paul Kei Matsuda. Mahwah, NJ: Lawrence Erlbaum Associates, 2001.

Assessment and Evaluation

Assessing Writing. Sara C. Weigle. Cambridge, UK: Cambridge University Press, 2002.

Assessing Second Language Writing in Academic Contexts. Ed. Liz Hamp-Lyons. Norwood, NJ: Ablex Publishing, 1991.

Response to Student Writing. Dana Ferris. Mahwah, NJ: Erlbaum, 2003.

Teacher Written Commentary in Second Language Writing Classrooms. Lynn M. Goldstein. Ann Arbor: University of Michigan Press, 2005.

Treatment of Error in Second Language Student Writing. Dana
R. Ferris. Ann Arbor: University of Michigan Press, 2002.
Writing across Borders (DVD). Oregon State University Writing
Intensive Curriculum & Oregon State University Center for
Writing and Learning (Producer) and Wayne Robertson,
(Writer/Director). United States: Oregon State University,
2005. (DVD available at cwl.oregonstate.edu/wab).

Designing or Teaching a Course for Second Language Writers

Teaching ESL Composition: Purpose, Process, and Practice.
Dana R. Ferris and John Hedgcock. (Second Ed.). Mahwah,
N.J.: Lawrence Erlbaum, 2005.
Teaching ESL Writing. Joy M. Reid. Englewood Cliffs, NJ: Prentice Hall Regents, 1993.
Teaching and Researching Writing. Ken Hyland. London: Pearson, 2002.
Writing Myths: Applying Second Language Research to Classroom Teaching. Joy Reid with Keith S. Folse, Cynthia M.
Schuemann, Pat Byrd and John Bunting, Ken Hyland, Dana
Ferris, Susan Conrad, Sharon Cavusgil, Paul Kei Matsuda. Ann
Arbor: University of Michigan Press, 2008.

Genres and Organization

Disciplinary Discourses: Social Interactions in Academic Writing.
Ken Hyland. Ann Arbor: University of Michigan Press, 2004.
Genre in the Classroom: Multiple Perspectives. Ed. Ann Johns.
Mahwah, NJ: Lawrence Erlbaum Associates, 2002.
Text, Role, and Context: Developing Academic Literacies. Ann
Johns. New York: Cambridge University Press, 1997.

Grammar

Explaining English Grammar. George Yule. Oxford: Oxford University Press, 1999.
*Grammar in the Composition Classroom: Essays on Teaching
ESL for College-Bound Students.* Pat Byrd and Joy M. Reid.
New York: Heinle & Heinle, 1998.

Keys to Teaching Grammar to English Language Learners: A Practical Handbook. Keith S. Folse. Ann Arbor: University of Michigan Press, 2009.

The Grammar Book: An ESL/EFL Teacher's Course. Marianne Celce-Murcia and Diane Larsen-Freeman. Boston: Heinle & Heinle, 1999.

Working with Graduate Students

Academic Writing for Graduate Students: Essential Tasks and Skills. John M. Swales and Christine B. Feak. (Second Edition). Ann Arbor: University of Michigan Press, 2004.

English in Today's Research World: A Writing Guide. John M. Swales and Christine B. Feak. Ann Arbor: University of Michigan Press, 2000.

Learning the Literacy Practices of Graduate School: Insiders' Reflections on Academic Enculturation. Eds. Christine Pearson Casanave and Xiaoming Li. Ann Arbor: University of Michigan Press, 2008.

Thesis and Dissertation Writing in a Second Language. Sue Starfield and Brian Paltridge. London: Routledge, 2007.

Research

A Synthesis of Research on L2 Writing in English. Ilona Leki, Alister Cumming, Tony Silva. London: Routledge, 2008.

Research on Composition: Multiple Perspectives on Two Decades of Change. Ed. Peter Smagorinsky. New York: Teachers College Press, 2006.

Understanding Second Language Writers

Critical Academic Writing and Multilingual Students. A. Suresh Canagarajah. Ann Arbor: University of Michigan Press, 2002.

Crossing the Curriculum: Multilingual Learners in College Classrooms. Eds. Vivian Zamel and Ruth Spack. Mahwah, NJ: Lawrence Erlbaum, 2004.

Generation 1.5 in College Composition: Teaching Academic Writing to U.S.-Educated Learners of ESL. Eds. Mark Roberge, Meryl Siegal, and Linda Harklau. London: Routledge, 2009.

How Languages are Learned. Patsy M. Lightbown and Nina Spada. (Third Edition). Oxford: Oxford University Press, 2006.

Undergraduates in a Second Language: Challenges and Complexities of Academic Literacy Development. Ilona Leki. London: Lawrence Erlbaum, 2007.

Understanding ESL Writers: A Guide for Teachers. Ilona Leki. Portsmouth, NH: Boynton/Cook Publishers, 1992.

Vocabulary

Vocabulary Myths: Applying Second Language Research to Classroom Teaching. Keith S. Folse. Ann Arbor: University of Michigan Press, 2004.

Teaching Vocabulary—Strategies and Techniques. I. S. P. Nation. Boston: Heinle ELT, 2008.

Websites

Dave's ESL Café. www.eslcafe.com

English as a Second Language (ESL) Resources, Handouts and Exercises. *OWL Online Writing Lab.* Purdue University. owl.english.purdue.edu/handouts/esl

Teachers of English to Speakers of Other Languages. www.tesol.org

Second Language Writing Interest Section (TESOL). second languagewriting.com/slwis

Symposium on Second Language Writing. sslw.asu.edu

Questions to Remember

1. What do I know about the student, the assignment, and the likely audience? (Chapters 1–3)

2. What does the student understand the goal of the paper to be? Could I figure out the goal just from reading the paper? Why or why not? (Chapters 3, 4)

3. As I read through the paper, are my expectations for what will come next met, or am I stopping and asking myself, "Why is the writer mentioning this here?" (Chapter 4)

4. Do I notice the usage of words and sentence patterns, or can I focus on meaning when I read? (Chapters 5, 6)

5. If I am primarily distracted by words and sentence patterns, is the issue the way the words and phrases are put together (Chapter 6), or do they just not sound right in this context (Chapter 5)?

6. Is punctuation or graphic design used to make the student's meaning clearer? (Chapter 7)

7. Am I making the interaction about more than just one paper? Am I taking advantage of opportunities to help the student become a better and more independent writer? (Chapter 8)